MSU LIBRARIES
W9-CCY-529

A Check List of Prose
Fiction Published in England
1740-1749

A Check List of Prose Fiction Published in England 1740-1749

Compiled by
Jerry C. Beasley

Published for the Bibliographical Society of
the University of Virginia

The University Press of Virginia
Charlottesville

THE UNIVERSITY PRESS OF VIRGINIA

First published 1972

ISBN: 0-8139-0401-3
Library of Congress Catalog Card Number: 72-75044
Printed in the United States of America

Contents

Introduction

The decade of the 1740's in England witnessed the sudden appearance of six remarkable works of fiction by three new artists named Samuel Richardson, Henry Fielding, and Tobias Smollett. These major novelists have justly received the close attention of scholars. Yet they appeared in company with a crowd of lesser fiction-writers whose efforts have enjoyed only the scantiest notice. The neglect of the minor native work is unquestionably justified if quality is made the main criterion of its interest, for most of it is trash. Nevertheless this forgotten literature makes up a very large part of the total picture of the decade's fiction, and in its time doubtless contributed greatly to the climate in which Richardson, Fielding, and Smollett achieved their first successes. It therefore deserves our notice.

The following check list attempts to provide as complete and systematic a record as possible of all the novels published in England during the years 1740-1749, including reprinted native works and foreign fiction in translation. In effect, it continues the effort of William Harlin McBurney, whose _A Check List of English Prose Fiction, 1700-1739_ (Cambridge: Harvard University Press, 1960) represents the most thorough attempt to recover and identify the works of fiction published in England during the four decades preceding _Pamela_. My own task of recovery has not been easy. The investigator who wants to learn about all the fiction published in the 1740's finds only a few very diverse modern aids to his search, all of them limited. The usefulness of Andrew Block's _The English Novel, 1740-1850: A Catalogue_ (London: William Dawson and Sons, 1961), the only bibliographical record that makes any attempt to cover the years in question, is severely qualified by the alphabetical arrangement of the listings, which are also incomplete. McBurney has compiled a list of _English Prose Fiction, 1700-1800, in the University of Illinois Library_ (Urbana: University of Illinois Press, 1965), and Sidney Gecker has edited a catalogue of _English Fiction to 1820 in the University of Pennsylvania Library_ (Philadelphia: University of Pennsylvania Press, 1954). These are helpful when supplemented with C. N. Greenough's "Catalogue of English Prose Fiction, 1470-1832," a card-index in Harvard University's Widener Library, and the shelf lists of the Newberry Library's Carpenter Collection of early English fiction. But all are incomplete, even in the aggregate.

No doubt my check list also commits sins of omission. The decade of the 1740's produced hundreds of novels, and inevitably some of them have escaped my net. However, the 338 entries I have compiled represent a very close approximation of the whole, and this record is far more comprehensive than any of the sources just mentioned, on which it was initially based. The information provided in those sources I have augmented (and sometimes corrected) by exploring the holdings of the British Museum and several American libraries, by examining the specialized listings and studies included in the bibliography, and by making full use of the Monthly Registers of new books found in the _Gentleman's_, _London_, and _Scots_ Magazines. In recording new books of all kinds that came to their attention, the editors of these magazines followed only crude methods of classification, and frequently confused fiction with other kinds of writing. Yet, the student who seeks the fullest possible picture of the fiction of the 1740's, apart from the works of Richardson, Fielding, Smollett, and a few other novelists, must have recourse to their listings.

In deciding upon standards of inclusion, I proceeded from several basic (if perhaps arbitrary) principles. The characteristically brief and discontinuous magazine fiction of the decade seemed clearly beyond my province, and besides has already received exhaustive attention in Robert D. Mayo's _The English Novel in the Magazines, 1740-1815_ (Evanston: Northwestern University Press, 1962). Moreover, as a general rule I omitted brief chapbooks, character sketches, jest books, and dialogues. There are exceptions, but usually such pieces do not develop as narratives, although they may have been aimed at the same audience that read long prose fiction. Finally, I excluded all works not published in the English language.

What remained after the application of these principles was an amorphous mass of narrative literature whose only recognizable features were the major novels of Richardson, Fielding, and Smollett, the works of a few lesser contemporaries like Eliza Haywood, Sarah Fielding, and Mary Collyer, and translations from such foreign novelists as Cervantes, Marivaux, and Prévost. In approaching this mass I adopted a liberal view of what is fiction and what is not. Works candidly calling themselves "novels" were easy to identify as imaginative literature, although to a contemporary reader the label "novel" signified little more than that a work was admittedly fictional, that it was probably a love story though it was not (or claimed not to be) a romance, and that it drew its subject and actions from familiar life, however implausible the handling of the narrative material might be. In the 1740's, however, most segments of the reading public still shared moral or literary biases against fictitious narrative that were hardly less intense than in the time of Addison or Defoe. The majority of contemporary novelists, although many of them were scribblers who cared little for either fiction or truth, yielded to popular prejudice and denied the fictional nature of their narratives, falsely protesting their "truth" instead.

Effective means of deception were readily at hand for such storytellers as cared to use them. The spirit of the early eighteenth century was vigorously anti-romantic, and

Englishmen of the day displayed an increasing interest in history, biography, and travel literature. Factual _lives_, _adventures_, _memoirs_, _letters_, _histories_, and _voyages_ were popular with readers of all kinds. These categories were easily appropriated by fiction-writers, who on the title pages of their books frequently made the same claims of authenticity as the authors of genuine memoirs and books of travel. Even inside, the factual is likely to be hard to separate from the fictional. The Aristotelian distinction between _real_ and _feigned_ history is easy enough to state, but frequently difficult to apply. Some stories are scrupulously true, no doubt, but others, though grounded on fact, so embellish and heighten the truth that it is nearly impossible to discriminate. Such productions are most properly regarded as at least marginal fiction. Indeed, in the absence of clear historical evidence to the contrary, I have classified as fiction any "history," "life," "voyage," or collection of letters that pursues a narrative line. Whatever their degree of authenticity, all "real," "true," and "factual" stories were competing for the attention of the same readers in the 1740's, and were obviously produced by writers with an eye on the marketplace.

The check list is organized by years, and works are entered according to the earliest verifiable date of appearance. The arrangement of all items named under a given year is alphabetical, and each new entry is numbered. Reprinted native pieces first published before 1740 I have designated by an asterisk (*) placed before the number of the entry. I have separated translations into a section at the end of the listing for each year. Translations reprinted from earlier years are also designated by an asterisk (*), and different translations of the same work are accorded separate entries by date of publication.

Individual entries record short titles only. Original spelling and punctuation are retained, but I have capitalized only first words and proper names; this policy seemed more sensible than trying to reproduce the endless variations in capitalization found on title pages. Following citation of the title, an entry usually provides these several kinds of supplementary information: the names of booksellers; the number of pages, or, in the case of multi-volume works, the number of volumes; the book format; the price, whenever known; the location (indicated in parentheses) of at least one extant copy, in an American library if possible. For reprints of both native works and translations I have usually given the original publication date, documented by reference to one of the sources listed in the bibliography or, when necessary, by mention of an existing library copy of the original edition. In the interest of continuity, I have in most such cases relied on McBurney's Check List, and have always referred to it if possible, either as a source or at the end of the whole citation. For every translation I have supplied, if available, the names of the author and translator, and the original title and date of publication.

Unless otherwise noted, dates of both native and translated works are from title pages, while the place of publication for native items is London, and that for the originals of translations from the French is Paris.

Subsequent editions of a work, through 1749, are mentioned under the first entry; a headnote to each year's entries provides cross references designed to make it possible to identify every item listed for a given year anywhere in the check list proper. Unverified editions of authentic works are included in Appendix A, and unauthenticated titles are listed in Appendix B. The brief descriptive annotations affixed to most entries are intended to suggest only in a general way the kind of work under consideration. Such annotations were of course not possible for the items in Appendix B; elsewhere, I have usually not thought it necessary to attempt this kind of description for the works of major authors.

In closing, I want to express my appreciation for all the courteous help I received at the many libraries where I have worked on this project. I would like especially to thank the directors and librarians of the Newberry Library and of the libraries of the University of Pennsylvania, Yale University, and Harvard University for very special kindnesses rendered. Finally I wish to thank the University of Delaware General Faculty Research Fund for financial support during the final stages of my work. To Professor Robert D.

Mayo, who saw me through the early stages and has patiently counseled me ever since, I am most deeply indebted.

University of Delaware

Newark, Delaware

Abbreviations

BM	British Museum
BPL	Boston Public Library
Bro	Brown University
C	Columbia University
CBEL	_Cambridge Bibliography of English Literature_
Chi	University of Chicago
Duk	Duke University
_GM_	_Gentleman's Magazine_
H	Harvard University
Hun	Huntington Library
I	University of Illinois
Ind	Indiana University
LC	Library of Congress
Leh	Lehigh University
_LM_	_London Magazine_
Mic	University of Michigan
N	Newberry Library
NCBEL	_New Cambridge Bibliography of English Literature_
NYPL	New York Public Library
P	University of Pennsylvania
Phil	Library Company of Philadelphia
Pri	Princteon University
Tex	University of Texas
UCLA	University of California, Los Angeles
Y	Yale University

A Check List of Prose Fiction Published in England 1740-1749

1740

See also below, Nos. 87 and 148.

1. An authentick account of the life of Mr Charles Drew.

Printed for J. Applebee. 48pp. 12mo. 6d. (H)

a. 1740. Second edition. 40pp. 8vo. (H)

b. 1740. The Suffolk Parricide.

Printed for J. Standen. 44pp. 8vo. (H)

Another issue of An authentick account, with a new title.

Routine, sensational criminal biography of a genuine youth executed for the brutal murder of his father.

2. The case of Mr. Bartholomew Greenwood submitted to the publick by himself.

Printed for T. Cooper. 55pp. 8vo. 1s. (LC)

A conventional narrative sketch recounting the criminal exploits of a glorified villain, and defending him against the "many Inconsistencies of Mr. Wheatley," one of his accusers.

3. Conversations moral and entertaining, between an English gentleman and a knight of Malta.
Printed for John Hawkins. 312pp. 12mo. (N; Duk; Ind)

a. 1743. Printed for J. Robinson. 312pp. 12mo. (H)

The frame-tale involves the friendship of a young Englishman Lactifer and a Maltese warrior; their eight conversations, on subjects ranging from education to reason and the passions, occasion several moralized novels and histoires.

4. The cruel mistress, being the genuine trial of E[liza]. B[ranch]. and her daughter.
Printed for J. Standen. 36pp. 12mo. 6d. (H)

a. 1740. Dublin: Printed for George Faulkner. 31pp. 12mo. (H)

b. 1740. An impartial relation of the barbarous murder committed by Mrs. Branch and her daughter.
Printed for T. Cooper. 6d. (Listed in GM June 1740).
Another issue of The cruel mistress, with a new title.

A sensational narrative recording the events leading up to and including the arrest and trial of two notorious female murderers, now penitent.

*5. The dangerous voyage of Capt. Thomas James, in his intended discovery of a northwest passage into the South-Sea. Printed for O. Payne. 142pp. 8vo. 2s.6d. (Y)

First published in 1633 as Captain Thomas James's strange and dangerous voyage (H).

a. 1741. Reprinted in Daniel Coxe's Collection of voyages and travels (see below, No. 50).

A fictionalized account of a daring, if unsuccessful, voyage by a genuine seventeenth-century explorer.

6. The devil of a story. Printed for T. Cooper. 24pp. 8vo. 6d. (N; Ind; Tex)

An allegorical tale about the evils of strong drink.

7. A faithful and full account of the surprizing life and adventures of the celebrated Doctor Sartorius Sinegradibus. Edinburgh: Printed for the author. 42pp. 8vo. (BM)

A satire of English high life using the adventures of the real-life John Taylor, a peripatetic and somewhat roguish surgeon-barber, who made a reputation ministering to the whims of fashionable people.

8. <u>The freaks of fortune; or, memoirs of Captain Conyers. A novel</u>.

Printed for C. Stalker. 186pp. 12mo. (N)

A sentimental love story telling of a benevolent young soldier whose love for a virtuous maiden is complicated first by his father's incestuous temptations, then by a series of mistaken identities, but finally is requited in happy marriage.

9. <u>A full and particular account of the life and notorious transactions of Roger Johnson . . . to the time of his death</u>.

Printed for C. Corbet. 27pp. 8vo. 6<u>d</u>. (BM)

Brief sketch of the life of a real rogue and criminal who, while in Newgate Prison, reformed and became a popular legal counsel to fellow inmates. Fielding drew upon this character for Book IV of <u>Jonathan Wild</u> (1743: below, No. 119).

10. <u>The history of Thomas Kouli Kan, Sophi of Persia</u>.

245pp. 12mo. (N)

See also below, Nos. B9 and B10.

a. 1747. (Listed in <u>GM</u> Sept. 1747).

This narrative, allegedly translated from the French, is a fictionalized account of the phenomenal rise of the Persian Nadir Kuli from robber chief to the Persian throne. He reigned until he was assassinated in 1747.

11. Injur'd innocence: or, the lives and surprizing adventures of Amicorus and Amicana. A true and modern story, wrote by a friend.
Second edition. 156pp. 12mo. (N)
No first edition known.

A sentimental novel about two impeccably virtuous lovers separated by the heroine's forced marriage of convenience to a rich old man, but inevitably brought together at last in a perfectly happy marriage of their own.

12. The life and adventures of Gilbert Langley . . . . Written by himself, in Maidstone-Goal [sic], when under condemnation for a robbery committed on the highway.
Printed by J. Applebee. 93pp. 8vo. 1s. (H)

This account of an apparently imaginary thief avoids the overt moralizing of conventional criminal biographies, and focuses on the personality of its subject, who becomes an engaging rogue-adventurer.

13. The life and adventures of Mrs. Christian Davies, the British Amazon, commonly called Mother Ross.

Printed for R. Montagu. 2 parts: 87, 104pp. 8vo. (H; P; Y)

See also below, No. 99.

(McBurney No. 332.)

a. 1741. Second edition. Printed for R. Montagu. 2 parts: 87, 104pp. 8vo. (I; N)

A Defoesque fictionalized account of the real Mother Ross, in autobiographical form. The heroine is a spirited, roguish woman who, in her youth, put on man's disguise and served bravely as a foot-soldier under Marlborough, earning his regard and the patronage of a great many people of quality.

14. The life and death of P[ierce] G[aveston] . . . . Prime Minister to . . . Edward II. . . . with political remarks . . . by a true patriot.

Printed for G. Bickham. 43pp. 8vo. 1s. (BM)

A fictionalized life of the favorite minister of Edward II of England, who ruled in the fourteenth century. Gaveston's greed and arrogance aroused the barons, who finally had him executed; a frontispiece to this book offers a portrait of Sir Robert Walpole, linking him to his ancient counterpart.

15. News from the dead, or a faithful and genuine narrative of an extraordinary combat between life and death, exemplified in the case of William Duell.
Printed for J. Roberts. 29pp. 8vo. (H)

The ghost-written sensational story of an imaginary rapist who is hanged at Tyburn but afterwards revives and dramatically repents of his crime.

16. A true and impartial history of the life and adventures of some-body.
Printed for Richard Higgins. 40pp. 8vo. (N)

A virulent satire of Sir Robert Walpole which attacks not his politics but his personal life, even alleging that his persecuted wife died from venereal disease communicated by him.

*17. Cooke, Alexander. A present for a papist: or, the history of the life of Pope Joan, from her birth to her death.
Printed for O. Payne. 88pp. 4to. 1s.6d. (C)
First published in 1675 (H).

Anti-Catholic diatribe couched in the spurious tale of a lascivious rambling female who went to Rome, assumed a male disguise as "John English" and became Pope, reigning as a man until one day she gave birth to a bastard and died while in solemn procession through the streets.

*18. Defoe, Daniel. The fortunate mistress: or, a history of the life and vast variety of fortunes of Mademoiselle de Beleau, . . . the Lady Roxana.
Printed by E. Applebee. 441pp. 4to. (N; Pri; UCLA)

Includes an anonymous, spurious continuation compiled in part from other works, including Eliza Haywood's novel The British recluse (1722: McBurney No. 131).

Roxana was first published in 1724 (Moore).
(McBurney No. 155.)

a. 1742. Printed for H. Slater. 346pp. 12mo. (Y)

This edition does not include the spurious continuation added in 1740.

b. 1745. The life and adventures of Roxana, the fortunate mistress; or, most unhappy wife.
Printed for C. Whitefield. 432pp. 12mo. (N)

Includes a new continuation, different from that of 1740, but also spurious.

19. Fielding, Henry [?]. An apology for the life of Mr. T . . . C . . . . , comedian. Being a proper sequel to the Apology for the life of Mr. Colley Cibber, comedian.
Printed for J. Mechell. 144pp. 8vo. 2s. (Y)

a. 1741. Dublin. (Y)

A burlesque autobiography often attributed to Henry Fielding but, according to Cross, not certainly his work.

*20. Haywood, Eliza. The city jilt; or, the Alderman turn'd beau. A secret history.
Printed by T. Bailey. 60pp. 8vo. (BM)
First published in 1726 (Whicher).
(McBurney No. 193.)

An amorous novel recounting the adventures of a sprightly heroine named Glicera who, beset by a lecherous old Alderman and a rakish young fop, triumphs over both by the use of her superior wits.

*21. Lediard, Thomas. The German spy: or, familiar letters from a gentleman on his travels thro' Germany, to his friend in England.

Second edition. Printed for T. Cooper. 436pp. 8vo. (N)
First published in 1738 (McBurney No. 326).

A "spy" narrative consisting of letters describing the principal cities and towns of Germany, with their political and ecclesiastical structures, and boasting of the "author's" acquisition of various magical devices by which he may measure the sense of man's speech, books, and philosophy.

22. Pennyman, Lady Margaret. _Miscellanies in prose and verse. With some other curious pieces_.
Printed for E. Curll. 112pp. 12mo. 3_s_. (N)

A collection including, besides occasional poems, three Italian _novelle_, an account of a journey to Paris, and several brief secret histories.

23. Richardson, Samuel. _Pamela: or, virtue rewarded_, Vols. I and II.
Printed for C. Rivington and J. Osborn. 2 vols. 12mo. 6_s_. (Y)
The title pages are dated 1741, although the work is widely known to have been actually published Nov. 6, 1740 (Sale).

See also below, No. 95, for Richardson's continuation in Vols. III and IV.

a. 1741. Dublin: Printed for George Faulkner and George Ewing. 2 vols. 12mo. 5s.6d. (Sale).

b. 1741. Second edition. Printed for C. Rivington and J. Osborn. 2 vols. 12mo. 6s. (Y)

c. 1741. Second Irish edition. Dublin: Printed for George Faulkner, George Ewing, and William Smith. 2 vols. 12mo. 5s.6d. (Sale).

d. 1741. Third edition. Printed for C. Rivington and J. Osborn. 2 vols. 12mo. 6s. (Y)

e. 1741. Fourth edition. Printed for C. Rivington and J. Osborn. 2 vols. 12mo. 6s. (I; Y)

f. 1741. Fifth edition. Printed for C. Rivington and J. Osborn. 2 vols. 12mo. 6s. (I; Y)

g. 1742. Sixth edition. Printed for S. Richardson. 2 vols. 8vo. (Y)

Published with Vols. III and IV, Third edition (see below, No. 95c). Price for the 4 vols., £1.4 (Sale).

TRANSLATIONS

*24. The right pleasant and diverting history of Fortunatus. Eleventh edition. Printed for J. Osborne. 12mo. (BM)

First published in English c.1650; the first dated English edition is that of 1676 (Mish).

This is the famous old sixteenth-century German story combining chivalric romance and circumstantial realism in the tale of a hero who, equipped by the goddess Fortune with the riches he has chosen from among her offered gifts, travels all over Europe and the Mediterranean before he learns that worldly goods alone do not bring happiness.

25. Aesopus. Aesop's fables. With instructive morals and reflections. . . . And the life of Aesop prefixed. Printed for J. Osborn. 192pp. 12mo. 2s.6d. (H)

Edited by Samuel Richardson, who also wrote the preface and the moral reflections following individual fables.

See also below, Nos. 68, 122, and 231.

a. 1747[?]. Second edition (Sale).

26. Argens, Jean Baptiste de Boyer, marquis d'. The Jewish spy: being a philosophical, historical and critical correspondence, by . . . certain Jews in Turky, Italy, France, &c.
Printed for D. Browne and R. Hett. 5 vols. 12mo. 3s. per vol. (I; P; Y)
Translated from Lettres juives (The Hague, 1736-1738). (McBurney No. 337.)

a. 1744. Second edition. Printed for D. Browne, R. Hett, J. Schuckburgh, etc. 5 vols. 12mo. (I; N)

b. 1746. Newcastle: Printed for James Fleming. 4 vols. 12mo. (H)

Like the same author's Chinese letters (translated 1741: below, No. 69), this is an imitation of Marana's popular Turkish spy (Twelfth English edition, 1748: below, No. 257); it presents an "alien" agent who writes letters home describing his own adventures and offering satirical observations on French society, politics, and religion.

*27. Cervantes Saavedra, Miguel de. The history of the valorous and witty knight-errant, Don Quixote de la Mancha.

Printed for D. Midwinter, W. Innys, R. Robinson, etc.
4 vols. 12mo. (BM)

This translation, by Thomas Shelton, was first published in 1612-1620 (Putnam).

Translated from El ingenioso hidalgo Don Quixote de la Mancha, 1605-1615.

See also below, Nos. 100, 123, 183, and A16.

a. 1747. 4 vols. 12mo. (BM)

*28. Fénelon, François de Salignac de la Mothe. The adventures of Telemachus, the son of Ulysses.
Printed for W. Innys, R. Manby, S. Birt, etc. 2 vols. 8vo. (H)

This is a new edition of the original English translation by Mr. Littlebury and Mr. Boyer, first published in 1699-1700 (N).

Translated from Suite du IVe livre d'Odyssée, ou les aventures de Télémaque, 1699-1700.

See also below, Nos. 103, 125, and 126.

a. 1742. Fifteenth edition. Printed for Brotherton, Innys, Meadows, etc. 5s.6d. (Listed in LM Dec. 1742).

Fénelon's famous didactic romance, or "prose epic" as Fielding called it in the Preface to Joseph Andrews (1742: below, No. 90), tells the story of young Telemachus's search for his father, and displays the lessons he learned from the wise teacher Mentor on the subject of how to be a good king. Télémaque was the most popular didactic romance of the eighteenth century, both in England and on the Continent.

*29. Gueulette, Thomas Simon. Chinese tales: or, the wonderful adventures of the Mandarin Fum-Hoam.
Second edition. Printed for J. Hodges. 236pp. 12mo. (I; N)

This translation, by the Rev. Thomas Stackhouse, was first published in 1725 (McBurney No. 186).

Translated from Les avantures merveilleuses du mandarin Fum Hoam. Contes chinois, 1723.

A sentimental pseudo-oriental imitation of Galland's Arabian nights (see below, No. 179). One of several successful works of this kind by Gueulette (see below, Nos. 128 and 278).

30. Mouhy, Charles de Fieux, Chevalier de. The fortunate country maid. Being the memoirs of the present celebrated Marchioness of L—— V——.

Printed for A. Dodd, 1740-1741. 4 parts: 2 vols. 12mo. 6s. (N; Y)

Translated from La paysanne parvenue, 1735-1737.

See also below, Nos. 107 and 160.

a. 1741. Second edition. Printed for F. Needham. 2 vols. 12mo. 6s. (Listed in LM Aug. 1741).

A loose translation of Mouhy's work, which was actually an imitation of Marivaux's Le paysan parvenu, 1734-1736. The story tells of an orphaned country girl who, through her perseverance in virtue, is finally rewarded with happy marriage and elevated social station. The obvious resemblances to Richardson's Pamela (1740: above, No. 23) may account for the attention the story received from English translators and adaptors.

*31. Olivier, J., Abbé. A continuation of the life and adventures of Signor Rozelli, late of The Hague. 12mo. (BM)

This continuation was first published in 1724, as a sequel to Memoirs of the life and adventures of Signor Rozelli, 1709 (McBurney Nos. 46 and 168).

Translated from Nouvelles avantures de l'infortune Napolitain, ou du Seigneur Rozelli (Amsterdam, 1721).

a. 1742. Another edition of the _Continuation_ (Stauffer).

A picaresque narrative recounting the adventures of a clever fellow who, having endured slavery, monasticism, the Inquisition, and mercurial revolutions of fortune, finally settles down to die. Often attributed to Defoe, but erroneously.

32. Tencin, Claudine Alexandria Guerin de. _The siege of Calais by Edward of England. An historical novel_. Printed for T. Woodward. 288pp. 12mo. 2_s_.6_d_. (P)
Translated from _Le siege de Calais, nouvelle historique_ (The Hague, 1740).

a. 1745. (_CBEL_).

b. 1748. (_CBEL_).

A sentimental love story written around familiar English and French history, and set in vaguely delineated fourteenth-century surroundings.

1741

See also above, Nos. 5, 13, 19, 23, and 30, and below, No. 270.

33. The British fratricide: being an exact and impartial narrative of the horrid . . . catastrophe of Sir John Dinely Goodere, Bart.
Printed by J. Hart. 31pp. 8vo. 6d. (BM)

A graphic, frenzied account of the murder of the Baronet by his brother Samuel. Samuel Foote, nephew to the victim, published in the same year a legitimate biography of his uncle entitled The genuine memoirs of the life of Sir John Dinely Goodere, Bart.

34. The confederacy: or, boarding school rapes.
Printed for E. Curll. 8vo. 2s.6d. (BM)

A sensational account of the escapades of Abraham Magny, John Crab, and others, climaxing in their trial for the brutal seduction and rape of a Mrs. Mary King.

35. A court intrigue; or, the statesman detected. A genuine story, delivered by the oraculous ship.

Printed for J. Huggonson. 48pp. 8vo. 1*s*. (H; N; Ind)

A narrative satire of Sir Robert Walpole's conduct during the early stages of the War of Jenkins' Ear.

36. A faithful narrative of the unfortunate adventures of Charles Cartwright, M.D., who in his voyage to Jamaica was taken by a Spanish privateer.
Printed for J. Roberts. 51pp. 8vo. 2*s*. (Y)

Published during the early stages of the War of Jenkins' Ear, this is a sensational account of an apparently imaginary ship's surgeon impressed aboard a Spanish vessel.

37. The history and adventures of Don Alphonso Blas De Lirias, son of Gil Blas of Santillane.
Printed for C. Ward, R. Chandler, J. Wood, etc. 294pp. 12mo. 2*s*.6*d*. (N; P)

a. 1742. Printed for James Hodges. 294pp. 12mo. (Y)

A spurious continuation of Le Sage's Gil Blas, 1715-1735 (see below, No. 105), which changes the emphasis of the original story, from active roguery to passive virtue.

*38. The ladies tales: exemplified in the vertues and vices of the quality, with reflections.

Third edition. Printed for Cooper. 12mo. (BM)

First published in 1714 (McBurney No. 70).

An "assembly" collection of brief amorous novels, moral *histoires*, and stories from the Bible, told to each other for their mutual amusement and edification by a group of travelers stranded at a country house after a stagecoach breakdown.

39. The life of Pamela.

Printed for C. Whitefield. 495pp. Alternate 8vo, 4to. (Y)

An elaborate retelling of Samuel Richardson's epistolary *Pamela* (1740: above, No. 23), cast into the form of a straightforward third-person narrative.

40. Memoirs of the life of Lady H—— the celebrated Pamela. From her birth to the present time.

Printed for T. Cooper. 67pp. 8vo. 1*s*. (H)

Written in response to Samuel Richardson's *Pamela* (1740: above, No. 23); according to Sale, the Lady H—— and

Sir A—— of this brief narrative are thinly disguised renderings of Sir Arthur and Lady Hesilrige, the alleged originals of Richardson's Pamela Andrews and Mr. B——.

41. A new journey to the world in the moon.
Second edition. Printed by C. Corbett. 84pp. 8vo. (I; N; Y; BPL; LC)

No first edition known.

An anti-Whig political satire featuring a "Lunar Philosopher" who recounts to an earthling visitor his own country's political and religious history of the past one hundred years. Because of its close resemblance to the Consolidator (1705: Moore; McBurney No. 17), this work was for a long time wrongly attributed to Daniel Defoe.

42. Pamela in high life; or, virtue rewarded.
Printed for Mary Kingman. 452pp. 12mo. (H; Mic)

A spurious continuation of Samuel Richardson's Pamela (1740: above, No. 23), possibly prompted by the first such fraud, Pamela's conduct in high life, by John Kelly (1741: below, No. 60). These two works appeared only months apart, and both carry the story of Richardson's heroine from her marriage all the way through to her death.

43. The secret history of Betty Ireland.
Printed for S. Lee. 37pp. 12mo. 6d. (Pri)

A salacious chapbook imitation of Defoe's earlier Moll Flanders and Roxana (see below, No. 52, and above, No. 18). This narrative was very popular; according to Stauffer, it enjoyed at least nine eighteenth-century editions.

44. The true account of the behaviour, confession, and dying words of James Hall, who was executed . . . for the barbarous murder of his master.
Printed for J. Huggonson. 8pp. 4to. (H)

The Newgate Ordinary's short fictionalized record of how James Hall, now dead but penitent, robbed and murdered his generous master John Penny.

45. "Cock, Samuel." A voyage to Lethe; by Capt. Samuel Cock; sometime commander of the good ship the Charming Sally.
Printed for J. Conybeare. 84pp. 8vo. (H; I)

A pornographic satirical narrative attacking conventional

morals, and leveling several burlesque charges at Pope and other eminent Augustans.

*46. Behn, Aphra. <u>All the histories and novels written by the late ingenious Mrs. Behn</u>.
Ninth edition. 2 vols. 12mo. (Bro)
This collection was first published in 1696 (Y).

a. 1744. (Greenough).

Includes, of course, the famous <u>Oroonoko</u>, along with Mrs. Behn's amorous novels and tales of scandal.

*47. Bunyan, John. <u>The pilgrim's progress from this world to the next</u>.
Printed for J. Clarke. 2 vols. 8vo. 5<u>s</u>. (H)
First published in two parts, 1678-1684 (Mish).

a. 1743. Printed for J. Clarke. 12mo. (BM)

b. 1744. Newcastle: Printed by John Gooding. 2 vols. 12mo. (H)

c. 1748. Printed for W. Johnstone. 12mo. (BM)

48. Chetwood, William Rufus. Five new novels.
Printed by W. Lewis. 104pp. 8vo. 2s.6d. (Y)
See also below, No. 89.

A collection of brief tales of amorous intrigue.

*49. ———. The voyages and adventures of Captain Robert Boyle, in several parts of the world.
Fifth edition. Dublin: Printed for George Golding. 308pp. 12mo. (H)
First published in 1726 (McBurney No. 191).

a. 1744. Liverpool: Printed by A. Sadler. 317pp. 12mo. (P; NYPL)

b. 1748. Sixth edition. Dublin. 312pp. 12mo. (P)

A very popular Defoesque imaginary voyage recounting the adventures of a courageous youth during his journey from England to the New World and back.

50. Coxe, Daniel, ed. A collection of voyages and travels. In three parts.
Printed for O. Payne. 142, 86, 122pp. 8vo. 5s. (P)

Includes a reprint of the 1740 edition of The dangerous voyage of Capt. Thomas James (see above, No. 5), along with a geographical description of Carolina and a military record of the French expedition to Carthagena in 1697.

51. Curll, Edmund. An impartial history of the life, character, amours, travels, and transactions of Mr. John Barber, City-Printer, Common-Councilman, Alderman, and Lord Mayor of London.
Printed for E. Curll. 48, 32pp. 8vo. 2s.6d. (N)

Curll's book, in part a reactin to Norton Defoe's Life and character of John Barber, Esq. (1741: below, No. 56), is a scathing narrative indictment of the late Alderman, which stretches truth in the interest of sensationalism. A "Last Will and Testament" and a group of the subject's letters are also included.

*52. Defoe, Daniel. The fortunes and misfortunes of the famous Moll Flanders.
Second edition. Printed for J. Brotherton, J. Stagg, and F. Noble. 324pp. 8vo. (H; BPL)
First published in 1722 (Moore).
(McBurney No. 128.)

*53. ————. The history and remarkable life of the truly honourable Colonel Jacque, vulgarly called Col. Jack.
251pp. 4to. (Pri)
First published in 1722 (Moore).
(McBurney No. 129.)

a. 1743. Sixth edition. Printed for Ward and Chandler. 363pp. 8vo. (BPL)

b. 1747. Sixth edition (Greenough).

*54. ————. A true and genuine history of the two last wars against France and Spain . . . . By Capt. George Carleton.
Printed for Francis Gosling. 352pp. 8vo. (I)
First published in 1728 (McBurney No. 230).

a. 1743. Memoirs of Capt. George Carleton, an English officer.
Printed for T. Astley. 352pp. 8vo. 4s. (I)

*55. ————. A true relation of the apparition of one Mrs. Veal, the next day after her death.
8vo. (BM)

First published in 1706 (Moore).

(McBurney No. 22.)

56. Defoe, Norton. The life and character of John Barber, Esq.; late Lord-Mayor of London.
Printed for T. Cooper. 60pp. 8vo. 1*s*. (BM)

a. 1742. Second edition. Printed for T. Cooper. 60pp. 8vo. (Greenough).

A whitewash biographical treatment of the late notorious printer (he died in 1740) who became alderman and Lord Mayor and who, as one of his feats, made the authoress Mrs. Mary Manley his mistress during the last years of her life. Edmund Curll's Impartial history . . . of Mr. John Barber (1741: above, No. 51) is an outraged reaction to this account.

57. Fielding, Henry. An apology for the life of Mrs. Shamela Andrews.
Printed for A. Dodd. 59pp. 8vo. 1*s*.6*d*. (I; Y)

a. 1741. Second edition. Printed for A. Dodd. 56pp. 8vo. (I; Y)

This is the most pointed and famous of all the many burlesques of Richardson's Pamela (1740: above, No. 23).

58. Haywood, Eliza [?]. Anti-Pamela: or, feign'd innocence detected; in a series of Syrena's adventures.
Printed for J. Huggonson. 281pp. 12mo. 2s.6d. (N)

a. 1742. Second edition. Printed for F. Cogan. 281pp. 12mo. (Boston Athenaeum Lib.)
Actually a second issue of the sheets of the first edition, but with a new title page (Sale).

After Fielding's Shamela (1741: above, No. 57), this is one of the most skillful of the parodies of Richardson's Pamela (1740: above, No. 23). Not certainly by Mrs. Haywood, but very possibly hers (Whicher).

*59. ————. The unfortunate princess, or, the ambitious statesman. Containing the life and surprising adventures of the princess of Ijaveo.
Printed for T. Wright. 224pp. 12mo. 2s. (C; N)
First published in 1736 as Adventures of Eovaai, Princess of Ijaveo (McBurney No. 313).

A pro-Jacobite orientalized political satire of Sir Robert Walpole, who is here characterized as a greedy lecher preying upon the kingdom and the virtue of a lovely young princess.

60. Kelly, John. Pamela's conduct in high life. Printed for Ward and Chandler. 2 vols. 12mo. 6s. (I: Vol. I only; N: Vol. I only; BM)

a. 1741. Dublin: Printed for G. Faulkner and O. Nelson. 312pp. 12mo. (P)
This is a reprint of Vol. I only of the London edition.

b. 1741. Second edition. Printed for Ward and Chandler. 2 vols. 12mo. 6s. (H)
Vol. I is truly a new edition; Vol. II of the first edition was combined with it when this edition was sold as a set in two volumes (Sale).

The first spurious continuation of Samuel Richardson's Pamela (1740: above, No. 23). An imitation of Kelly's fraud appeared within months, Pamela in high life (1741: above, No. 42). Both continuations carry the story of Pamela through to her death; Kelly's probably did most to prompt

Richardson's own continuation, the authentic third and fourth volumes of Pamela (Sale).

61. Lyttleton, George. The court-secret: a melancholy truth. Now first translated from the original Arabic.
Printed for T. Cooper. 50pp. 8vo. 1s. (I; N)

a. 1742. Printed for T. Cooper. 43pp. 8vo. (BM)

b. 1743. Printed for T. Cooper. 47pp. 8vo. (I)

An orientalized political fable which satirizes Sir Robert Walpole's behavior during the early months of the War of Jenkins' Ear, and even suggests that the Prime Minister had a part in driving the Patriot Opposition's Earl of Scarborough to suicide.

*62. Manley, Mary de la Rivière. The power of love: in seven novels.
Printed for C. Davis. 368pp. 8vo. (I; N)
First published in 1720 (McBurney No. 115).

Most of these seven mildly sentimental tales of passion are derived from Bandello through William Painter's Palace of pleasure (1566), but two, "The physician's stratagem" and "The perjur'd beauty," are original imitations by Mrs. Manley.

63. Parry, James. The true anti-Pamela: or, memoirs of Mr. James Parry, late organist of Ross in Hertfordshire. Printed for the author. 275, 98pp. 12mo. 3s. (Y)

a. 1741. Printed for the author. 418pp. 12mo. (Y)
According to Sale, a pirated edition.

b. 1741[?]. Dublin: Printed for Thomas Armitage. 12mo. (Sale).
According to Sale, probably copied from the pirated London edition of 1741.

c. 1742. Second edition. Printed for the author. 359pp. 12mo. 3s. (P)

Parry's book trades on the currency of Richardson's Pamela (1740: above, No. 23) and Mrs. Haywood's Anti-Pamela (1741: above, No. 58); it reverses Richardson's story, and tells the tale of its author's alleged entanglement with a young woman of fortune and position, who ruined him after making false promises of marriage.

64. Povey, Charles. <u>The virgin in Eden: or, the state of innocency</u>.
Printed by J. Roberts. 118pp. 8vo. 1<u>s</u>.6<u>d</u>. (I; N)

a. 1741. Second edition. Printed by J. Roberts. 118pp. 8vo. (Sale).

Through various parables, and especially through the joined stories of a nobleman, a student, and an heiress, all on their way from Sodom to Canaan, this book sets out to expose what its author sees as the false and inflammatory nature of Richardson's <u>Pamela</u> (1740: above, No. 23).

*65. Rowe, Elizabeth Singer. <u>Friendship in death: in twenty letters from the dead to the living. To which are added, Letters moral and entertaining, in prose and verse. In three parts</u>.
Printed for H. Lintot. 472pp. 8vo. (N)
First published in 1728-1732 (McBurney No. 234).

a. 1743. Printed for H. Lintot. 472pp. 8vo. (I)

b. 1745. Printed for H. Lintot. 472pp. 8vo. (I)

c. 1746. Printed for H. Lintot. 2 vols. 12mo. (I)

The brief epistolary tales gathered in Mrs. Rowe's extremely popular works are all calculated to "impress the Notion of the Soul's Immortality." As pious fictions by a celebrated lady, they were enormously influential in the 1730's and 1740's.

*66. Swift, Jonathan. A tale of a tub.
Eighth edition. Dublin: Printed for W. Smith and G. Faulkner. 264pp. 12mo. (P)

First published in 1704 (Teerink).

(McBurney No. 13.)

a. 1743. Tenth edition. Printed for C. Bathurst. 220pp. 12mo. (I; P)

b. 1747. Eleventh edition. Printed for C. Bathurst. 220pp. 12mo. (P)

67. Wilford, John. Memorials and characters, together with the lives of divers eminent and worthy persons.
Printed for J. Wilford. 788, 42pp. 8vo. (H)

A massive collection of about 200 exaggerated sketches of virtuous lives, adapted chiefly from funeral sermons preached over the remains of exemplary nobility, gentry, and clergy.

TRANSLATIONS

68. Aesopus. Aesop's fables. With their morals. Printed for J. Hodges. 12mo. (BM)

This is not the similarly titled Richardson edition (1740: above, No. 25), but another.

See also below, Nos. 122 and 231.

69. Argens, Jean Baptiste de Boyer, marquis d'. Chinese letters. Printed for D. Browne and R. Hett. 314pp. 12mo. 3s. (I; P; Y)

Translated from Lettres chinoises, 1739-1740.

a. 1743. Printed for R. Hett. 12mo. 3s. (Listed in GM Dec. 1743).

Like the same author's Jewish spy (translated 1739-1740: above, No. 26), this is an imitation of Marana's Turkish spy (Twelfth English edition, 1748: below, No. 257).

*70 Aulnoy, Marie Catherine Jumelle de Berneville, comtesse d'. The history of Hypolitus, Earl of Douglas. With the secret history of Macbeth, King of Scotland. To which is added, The art of love, or the amours of Count Schlick and a young lady of quality.

Printed for H. Slater, F. Noble, J. Rowland, etc. 362pp. 12mo. (P)

This translation first appeared in 1708 (McBurney No. 35).

Translated from Les avantures d'Hypolite, comte de Douglas . . . , 1690.

The stories of Hypolitus and Macbeth romanticize popular English history; the tale of Count Schlick is a scandal narrative about more recent French court life.

71. Boccaccio, Giovanni. The decameron, or ten days entertainment of Boccace.

Printed for R. Dodsley. 591pp. 8vo. 6s. (H)

Translated from the Decamerone, c.1353.

*72. Cervantes Saavedra, Miguel de. Persiles and Sigismunda. A novel.

Printed for C. Ward, R. Chandler, J. Wood, etc. 2 vols. 12mo. 5s. (BM)

First translated in 1619 as <u>The travels of Persiles and Sigismunda</u> (N).

Translated from the verse romance, <u>Los trabaios de Persiles y Sigismunda</u>, 1617.

a. 1745. Printed for T. Wright. 2 vols. 12mo. (I; P; Y)

73. ———. <u>Two humourous novels</u>.

Printed for Ward and Chandler. 183pp. 12mo. 2<u>s</u>. (H; N; Y)

Extracted and translated from <u>Novelas exemplares</u>, 1613.

a. 1742. Printed for William Sandby. 183pp. 12mo. (I)

The quasi-picaresque tales of "El coloquio de los perros" and "Rinconete and Cortadillo" are two of the non-amorous satirical tales omitted from all early English editions of the <u>Novelas exemplares</u> (see below, No. 124).

74. Crébillon, Claude Prosper Jolyot de. <u>The sofa: a moral tale</u>.

Printed for T. Cooper. 2 vols. in 1. 12mo. 3<u>s</u>. (NYPL; UCLA)

Translated from <u>Le sopha, conte moral</u>, 1740.

A satirical attack on the Court of Louis XV, this story tells how the spirit of a virtuous youth is imprisoned in a sofa, where it "witnesses" the depravity of Court figures pursuing their animal desires, finally to be released when two virtuous, sincere lovers appear and join in a union of love.

*75. Fontanieu, Gaspard Moise de. Rosalinda, a novel. Second edition. Printed for J. Osborn. 347pp. 8vo. (I)

This translation was first published in 1733 (McBurney No. 285).

Translated from Rosalinde, imitée de l'Italienne de Bernardo Morando (Grenoble and The Hague, 1730).

The heroic adventures of Edmund, Earl of Salisbury under England's Charles I, form the background of this pro-Catholic didactic romance, which takes its hero all across Europe in quest of a lady who does not love him. The Parliamentary Wars, Barbary slave-traders, and African deserts also figure in the lives of the hero and heroine.

*76. Le Sage, Alain René. Le diable boiteux; or, the devil upon two sticks.

Seventh edition. Printed for J. and R. Tonson. 2 vols. 12mo. (I)

This translation was first published in 1708 (McBurney No. 38).

Translated from <u>Le diable boiteux</u>, 1707.

The once-famous story of Don Cleophus, who one day accidentally released the demon Asmodeus from a bottle where he had been imprisoned by an astrologer. Asmodeus accompanies the Don through "Madrid," lifts the roofs off of houses, and exposes what is within in the form of satirical novels.

77. Marivaux, Pierre de Carlet de Chamblain. <u>The life of Marianne; or, the adventures of the Countess of ***</u>. Printed for C. Davis, 1736, 1741, 1742. 3 vols. 12mo. 2<u>s</u>.6<u>d</u>. (I)

Translated from <u>La vie de Marianne</u>, 1731-1741.

See also below, Nos. 129 and 212.

(McBurney No. 318.)

a. 1742. Dublin: Printed for G. Faulkner, W. Heatly, and O. Nelson. 2 vols. 8vo. (N)

b. 1743. Second edition. Printed for Charles Davis and Paul Vaillant. 2 vols. 12mo. (I)

c. 1744. 2 vols. 12mo. (Greenough).

78. Prévost d'Exiles, Antoine Francois, Abbé. The history of a fair Greek, who was taken out of a seraglio at Constantinople.

Printed for J. Roberts. 2 vols. 12mo. 5s. (N; P)

Translated from Histoire d'une Grecque moderne, 1741.

A passionate, partially orientalized novel about a virtuous maiden rescued from the clutches of a lusty Ottoman Emperor and brought to Paris. There the narrator falls hopelessly in love with her upon learning of her adventures, and hearing her tell the sad tales of several other "slaves."

*79. ———. The life and entertaining adventures of Mr. Cleveland, natural son of Oliver Cromwell, written by himself.

Printed for T. Astley. 3 vols. 12mo. 7s.6d. (LC)

This translation was first published in 5 vols., 1734-1735 (McBurney No. 265).

Translated from <u>Le philosophe anglais, ou l'histoire de Mr. Cleveland, fils naturel de Cromwel</u>, 1731-1739.

*80. ———. <u>Memoirs of a man of quality</u>.
Printed for J. Wilford and E. Cave, 1741-1742. 2 vols. 12mo. 3<u>s</u>., 3<u>s</u>.6<u>d</u>. (N)

Vol. I of this translation was first published in 1738 (McBurney No. 327).

Translated from <u>Mémoires d'un homme de qualité</u>, 1728-1731.

See also below, No. 130, for a rival translation.

a. 1744. (Listed in <u>GM</u> July 1744).

81. Saumery, Pierre Lambert de. <u>The devil turn'd hermit: or, the adventures of Astaroth banish'd from Hell</u>.
Printed for J. Hodges, J. Robinson, J. Wilcox, etc., 1741-1742. 2 vols. 12mo. 2<u>s</u>.6<u>d</u>. (N)

Translated from <u>Le diable hermite, ou avantures d'Astaroth banni des enfers</u> (Amsterdam, 1741).

a. 1744. (Greenough).

This satirical romance includes conversations between the the author and the banished demon Astaroth, and incorporates secret histories of French Court life, as well as scandalous stories of monks and nuns. It is an imitation of Le Sage's _Le diable boiteux_ (see above, No. 76).

*82. Scarron, Paul. _The whole comical works of Mr. Scarron._ Fifth edition. 2 vols. 12mo. 6_s_. (H)

This collection was first published in 1700 (McBurney No. 5).

Includes the famous _Roman comique_, 1651, along with various other novels and _histoires_.

1742

See also above, Nos. 18, 23, 28, 31, 37, 56, 58, 61, 63, 73, and 77, and below, No. 278.

83. _Account of the life, adventures and transactions of Robert Ramsey, alias Sir Robert Gray_.
38pp. 8vo. (BM)

Routine narrative of the escapades of a notorious forger and robber, including his apprehension, trial, and execution. Allegedly collected from the account supplied by the criminal's brother, John Ramsey.

84. <u>Memoirs of the nobility, gentry, &c. of Thule: or, the island of love</u>.

Printed for W. Webb, 1742-1744. 2 vols. 12mo. (H; Y)

a. 1744. Second edition. Printed for W. Webb. 2 vols. 12mo. 6<u>s</u>. (N)

b. 1746. 2 vols. 5<u>s</u>. (Listed in <u>GM</u> April 1746).

A frame-tale recording the experiences of a young virtuous lady named Aloisa, who has arrived in Thule (that is, England) in quest of a family legacy, occasions glimpses of all strata of Thulean society, and encloses secret histories purporting to expose all its established institutions and the people who run them, including the government and the Church.

85. <u>The settee; or Chevalier Commodo's metamorphosis. By Monsieur de *****. Done from the French</u>.

51pp. 8vo. (N)

A brief native imitation of Crébillon <u>fils</u>' <u>The sofa</u> (see above, No. 74).

86. *The silph's resentment; or, the Numidian coquet: a satyrical novel*.
Printed for T. Cooper. 29pp. 4to. 6*d*. (P)

A brief satirical narrative directed at George II and his various mistresses.

*87. "Zelis the Persian." *Celenia and Adrastes; with the delightful history of Hyempsal, king of Numidia: an allegorical romance*.
Dublin: Printed for Cor. Wynne. 2 vols. 12mo. (N)
First published complete in 1736 (McBurney No. 314); the first half of *Celenia* originally appeared in *The Persian letters continued*, 1735 (Fifth edition, 1744: below, No. 138).

a. 1740. Printed for R. Hodges. 2 vols. 8vo. (Greenough).

A mini-heroic romance adapted to the uses of political controversy, this work adopts a Tory-Jacobite position from which it attacks Sir Robert Walpole and the ruling Whig oligarchy.

88. Carey, Henry. _Cupid and Hymen; or, a voyage to the isles of love and matrimony. Containing a most diverting account of the inhabitants of those two vast and populous countries, their laws, customs, and government._
Printed for M. Cooper. 48, 45pp. 12mo. 2s. (N)

a. 1748. 12mo. (BM)

These little pieces parody the typical utopian voyage narrative, but also stand as satirical "allegories of love" exploding received notions of courtship and arranged marriage.

89. Chetwood, William Rufus. _The twins; or, the female traveller._
Printed for W. Chetwood, 1742-1743. 48pp. 8vo. (BM)
Reprinted from Chetwood's _Five new novels_ (1741: above, No. 48).

A brief tale of amorous intrigue, involving the comedy of sexual disguises, and the consequent confusion of identity.

90. Fielding, Henry. _The history of the adventures of Joseph Andrews, and of his friend Mr. Abraham Adams._

Printed for A. Millar. 2 vols. 12mo. 6s. (I; P; Y)

a. 1742. Second edition. Printed for A. Millar. 2 vols. 12mo. 6s. (I; Y)

b. 1742. Dublin. (Cross).

c. 1743. Third edition. Printed for A. Millar. 2 vols. 12mo. 6s. (I; P; Y)

d. 1747. Dublin. (Cross).

e. 1749. Fourth edition. Printed for A. Millar. 2 vols. 12mo. (I; Y)

*91. Haywood, Eliza. Secret histories, novels, and poems. Fourth edition. Printed for R. Ware, S. Birt, D. Browne, etc. 4 vols. 12mo. (I; P)

First published in 1725 (Whicher).

(McBurney No. 179.)

A collection of Mrs. Haywood's early novels of tender passion, together with her *chroniques scandaleuses* and occasional poems.

*92. Johnson, Captain Charles. <u>A general history of the lives and adventures of the most famous highwaymen</u>.
Printed for R. Walker. 427pp. 4to. (H)
First published in this form in 1734 (McBurney No. 68e).

A collection of brief narrative sketches of a multitude of genuine rogues, whose glamorous adventures have been especially selected to divert and instruct the public.

93. Lyttleton, George. <u>The affecting case of the queen of Hungary, in relation to both friends and foes; a fair specimen of modern history, by the author of The court secret</u>.
Printed for T. Cooper. 45pp. 8vo. (Y)

Satire of the English government's slippery relationships with Continental allies during the early stages of the War of Jenkins' Ear. Not so virulent as <u>The court secret</u> (1741: above, No. 61).

94. Manning, Robert. <u>Moral entertainments on the most important points of the Christian religion</u>.
Printed for Robinson and Pemberton. 3 vols. 12mo. 9<u>s</u>.
(BM)

Brief moral fables, some adapted from biblical stories, and all designed to illustrate various points of orthodox Anglican doctrine.

95. Richardson, Samuel. Pamela: or, virtue rewarded, Vols. III and IV.
Printed for S. Richardson. 2 vols. 12mo. 6s. (H; I; Y)
Richardson continued his original story of Pamela (1740: above, No. 23) in these new volumes.

a. 1742. Dublin: Printed for George Faulkner, George Ewing, and William Smith. 2 vols. 12mo. (Sale).
According to Sale, a pirated edition.

b. 1742. Second edition. Printed for S. Richardson. 2 vols. 12mo. 6s. (I)

c. 1742. Third edition. Printed for S. Richardson. 2 vols. 8vo. (Y)
Published with Vols. I and II, Sixth edition (see above, No. 23g). Price for the 4 vols., £1.4 (Sale).

*96. Swift, Jonathan. The history of Martin. Being a proper sequel to The tale of a tub.

Printed for T. Taylor. 24pp. 8vo. (H; Y)

First published separately from the _Tale_ (1704) in 1720 (Teerink).

Originally inserted in the _Tale_ (see above, No. 66) under the title "What follows after Section IX. in the Manuscript," this almost nonsensical narrative composed of phrases resembling chapter-heads was separated and issued as a satirical spin-off from the longer work.

*97. ————. _Travels into several remote nations of the world. In four parts. By Lemuel Gulliver_.

Printed for C. Bathurst. 351pp. 12mo. (I)

First published by Benjamin Motte in 1726 (Teerink). (McBurney No. 199.)

a. 1747. Fifth edition of the original version of 1726. Printed for C. Bathurst. 269pp. 12mo. (I)

b. 1748. 2 vols. 12mo. (P)

*98. Taylor, Jeremy. _The history of the life and death of the holy Jesus; with the lives, acts, and martyrdoms of his apostles_.

Tenth edition. 2 vols. (Phil)

First published in 1649 (CBEL).

An imaginative, impassioned rendering in prose narrative of the life of Jesus, by the man whom eighteenth-century admirers were fond of calling the "Shakespeare of divines."

99. Wilson, J. The British heroine: or, an abridgement of The life and adventures of Mrs. Christian Davies, commonly call'd Mother Ross . . . by J. Wilson, formerly a surgeon in the army.
179pp. 8vo. (C)

a. 1744. Second edition. 8vo. (BM)

This spurious spin-off from The life and adventures of Mrs. Christian Davies (1740: above, No. 13) reduces the original circumstantial narrative to the level of the incredible.

TRANSLATIONS

100. Cervantes Saavedra, Miguel de. The life and exploits of the ingenious gentleman Don Quixote de la Mancha.
Printed for J. and R. Tonson. 2 vols. 4to. 2 guineas.
(N; P)

A new translation by Charles Jarvis.

See also above, No. 27, and below, Nos. 123 and A16.

a. 1747. Dublin. 4 vols. 12mo. (P)

b. 1749. Second edition. Printed for J. and R. Tonson, and R. Dodsley. 2 vols. 8vo. 12*s*. (Y)

*101. Chansierges, Mr. *Grecian tales: or, the entertaining adventures of Neoptolemus, son of Achilles*.
Printed for W. Webb. 202pp. 12mo. 2*s*. (P)

This translation probably first appeared in 1724 (McBurney No. X15).

Translated from *Les avantures de Néoptolème, fils d'Achille* (Paris, 1718; and The Hague, 1719).

An imitation of Fénelon's great didactic romance of *Télémaque* (see above, No. 28).

*102. Crébillon, Claude Prosper Jolyot de. *The skimmer; or, the history of Tanzai and Neadarne*.
Printed for F. Galicke. 2 vols. in 1. 12mo. (I)

This translation was first published in 1735 (McBurney No. 305).

Translated from Tanzai et Néadarne, histoire japonaise, 1734.

a. 1748. 12mo. (BM)

A licentious orientalized satire of the Courts of Louis XIV and XV of France, this tale shows how young Tanzai (Louis XV) was required by a fairy princess to make an old woman (France, and the French Catholic Church) swallow a skimmer (the Papal Bull Unigenitus) before he could marry.

103. Fénelon, Francois de Salignac de la Mothe. The adventures of Telemachus.
Printed for J. Gray. 2 vols. 12mo. 6s. (Phil)
A new bilingual edition by Mr. Des Maizeaux.
See also above, No. 28, and below, Nos. 125 and 126.

104. Holberg, Ludwig, Baron. A journey to the world under-ground, by Nicholas Klimius.
Printed for T. Astley. 324pp. 12mo. 3s. (I; N; P)
Translated from Nicolai Klimii iter subterraneum, c.1730.

a. 1746. (Greenough).

The Danish Baron Holberg's imitation of Swift's Gulliver's Travels (see above, No. 97) tells the autobiographical story of a young student who falls into the center of the earth where he finds another world of Swiftean nations and creatures, all of which become vehicles of satirical commentary on the real world. According to Gove, the Journey enjoyed thirty-four European editions in the eighteenth century.

*105. Le Sage, Alain René. The history and adventures of Gil Blas of Santillane, Vol. IV.
Printed for J. Nourse. 346pp. 12mo. 3s. (BM)
Vol. IV of this translation was first published in 1735, Vols. I-III in 1716-1725 (McBurney No. 85).
Translated from Histoire de Gil Blas de Santillane, 1715-1735.
See also below, Nos. 182, 280, and A17.

a. 1744. Fifth edition. Printed for J. and R. Tonson. 3 vols. 12mo. (P)

b. 1746. Printed for J. Nourse and M. Cooper. 4 vols. 12mo. (BM)
Vols. I-III are a reissue of the Fifth edition of 1744; Vol. IV is dated 1746.

106. Mouhy, Charles de Fieux, Chevalier de. The busy-body: or, successful spy: being the entertaining history of Mons. Bigand.
Printed for F. Cogan. 2 vols. 12mo. 6s. (I; N; P; Y)
Translated, possibly by Eliza Haywood (Whicher), from La mouche, ou les avantures de M. Bigand, 1736.

a. 174[?]. Dublin: Printed for James Hoey. 2 vols. 12mo. (P)

Picaresque tale of a tiny rogue whose size throws him into many odd adventures, and makes it possible for him to "spy" on all manner of people. This imitation of Le Sage remains Mouhy's best-known work.

107. ———. The virtuous villager, or virgin's victory.
Printed for F. Cogan. 2 vols. 12mo. (N; Y)
Translated by Eliza Haywood from La paysanne parvenue, 1735-1737.
For a rival translation see above, No. 30.

108. Prévost d'Exiles, Antoine Francois, Abbé. The dean of Coleraine. A moral history, founded on the memoirs of an illustrious family in Ireland.

Printed for T. Cooper, 1742-1743. 3 vols. 12mo. 6*s*. (I)

Translated from *Le doyen de Killerine, histoire morale*, 1735.

*109. Quevedo y Villegas, Francisco Gomez de. *The comical works of Don Francisco de Quevedo*.

Printed for C. Ward, R. Chandler, and W. Sandby. 352pp. 12mo. 3*s*.6*d*. (P; Y)

This translation, by John Stevens, was first published in 1707 (Esdaile).

See also below, No. 187.

This collection includes the picaresque novel *Paul, the Spanish sharper*, better known as *El buscón* (1626), and the series of nine brief satirical episodes called *The night-adventurer*.

1743

See also above, Nos. 3, 47, 53, 54, 61, 65, 66, 69, 77, and 90, and below, Nos. 187 and 233.

110. *The modern miscellany. In three parts*.

Printed for Will's o' Wisp. 3 vols. in 1. 12mo. (N)

Contains, along with some meditations and devotional poems, a fictionalized confessional autobiography by a reputed conjurer named Richard Walton.

111. "Kapha, Belshazzar, the Jew." The book of the chronicle of James, the nephew . . . . translated from the original Arabic.
Printed for J. Warner. 30pp. 8vo. (BM)

An allegorical pamphlet narrative in support of James Annesley's claim to nobility, which Annesley's own Memoirs of an unfortunate young nobleman (1743-1747: below, No. 113) treats at much greater length.

112. "Quevedo, Don, Junior." A particular account of Cardinal Fleury's journey to the other world.
Printed for W. Webb. 78pp. 8vo. (BM)

A satirical narrative sometimes erroneously attributed to Henry Fielding, according to Cross, who also suggests that the work may have been inspired by Fielding's A journey from this world to the next (Vol. II of the Miscellanies, 1743: below, No. 119).

113. Annesley, James. Memoirs of an unfortunate young nobleman, return'd from a thirteen years slavery in America.

Printed for J. Freeman. 2 vols. 12mo. 3s. per vol. (I; N; Y)

See also below, No. 135, for a plagiarism of this work.

a. 1747. Vol. III. 12mo. 2s. (Y)

This is Annesley's fictionalized account of his unsuccessful attempts to gain a title which he claimed his uncle Richard, the Earl of Anglesey, had usurped after selling him into American slavery. This famous case was later treated by Tobias Smollett in Chapter CVI of The adventures of Peregrine Pickle, 1751.

114. Bulkeley, John. A voyage to the South-Seas, in the years 1740-1.

Printed for J. Robinson. 220pp. 8vo. (Y)

A sensational account of an English military expedition, during which a ship called the *Wager* was lost to the enemy in battle.

115. Collyer, Mary. *Memoirs of the Countess de Bressol*. Printed for Jacob Robinson. 2 vols. 12mo. 6*s*. (I)

Allegedly done from the French, but apparently an original sentimental novel in imitation of Marivaux, by one of his most capable translators (see below, No. 129).

*116. Congreve, William. *Incognita: or, love and duty reconciled. A novel*.
Dublin: Printed for Joseph Rhames. 62pp. (Ind)
First published in 1692 (Mish).

This is Congreve's famous pioneering "dramatic novel" of love and intrigue.

*117. Defoe, Daniel. *The pleasant, and surprizing adventures of Mr. Robert Drury*.
Printed for W. Meadows. 470pp. 8vo. (I)

First published in 1729 as _Madagascar; or, Robert Drury's journal_ (Moore).
(McBurney No. 241.)

a. 1747. _The adventures of Mr Robert Drury during his 15 years captivity in Madagascar_.
Printed for J. Robinson. 5_s_. (Listed in _GM_ April 1747).

118. Erskine, William. _The travels and adventures of Mademoiselle de Richelieu, cousin to the present Duke of that name, who made the tour of Europe dressed in man's cloaths attended by her maid Lucy as her valet de chambre_. Dublin: Printed for O. Nelson. 3 vols. 12mo. (N)
See also below, No. 238, for a plagiarism of this work.

a. 1744. Printed for A. Cooper. 3 vols. 12mo. 9_s_. (H; P)

b. 1744. Dublin. 3 vols. 12mo. (Greenough).

A quasi-picaresque tale of a young woman's travels across Europe, and of the comical adventures arising from her disguise. The story is anti-French and anti-Catholic in its satire.

119. Fielding, Henry. Miscellanies.
Printed for the author, and sold by A. Millar. 3 vols. 8vo. (I; Y)

a. 1743. Second edition. Printed for A. Millar. 3 vols. 8vo. (I; Y)

b. 1743. Dublin. (Cross).

Includes A journey from this world to the next (Vol. II), and The life of Mr. Jonathan Wild the great (Vol. III).

*120. Manley, Mary de la Rivière. The secret history of Queen Zarah, and the Zarazians.
Printed for J. Huggonson. 95pp. 8vo. 1s.6d. (I)
First published in 1705 (McBurney No. 18).

a. 1745. Fourth edition. Printed for J. Wilford. 95pp. 4to. 1s. (BM)

b. 1749. Fifth edition. Printed by J. Towland, W. Mynard, and J. Wren. 95pp. 4to. (Greenough).

This is a Tory defender's orientalized satirical attack on Sarah Churchill, Duchess of Marlborough and confidante of Queen Anne.

TRANSLATIONS

121. Memoirs of the love and state-intrigues of the court of H——. From the marriage of the Princess of Z—— to the tragical death of Count K——k.
Printed for J. Huggonson. 119pp. 8vo. 1s.6d. (H; I; P)

a. 1744 [?]. Second edition. Printed for J. Robinson. 119pp. 8vo. (BM)

Based on real events and possibly written by the German Countess of Konigsmarck, this lively, romanticized narrative defends the Princess of Zelle who, unhappy with her marriage into the House of Hanover, had become entangled with the gallant young Count of Konigsmarck; his death was demanded as retribution.

*122. Aesopus. Aesop naturaliz'd: in a collection of fables and stories from Aesop, Locman, Pilpay and others.
Fifth edition. Printed for D. Midwinter and A. Ward. 160pp. 8vo. (I)

An alleged third edition of this version of Aesop had appeared in 1711 (I).

See also above, Nos. 25 and 68, and below, No. 231.

*123. Cervantes Saavedra, Miguel de. <u>The history of the renown'd Don Quixote de la Mancha</u>.
Seventh edition. 4 vols. 12mo. 12s. (Y)

This translation, by Peter Motteux, was first published in 1700, and revised in 1725 by John Ozell (Putnam).

See also above, Nos. 27 and 100, and below, No. A16.

a. 1744. Seventh edition (another issue). Printed for D. Midwinter, W. Innys, R. Ware, etc. 4 vols. 12mo. (BM)

b. 1749. Printed for W. Innys, R. Ware, S. Birt, etc. 4 vols. 12mo. (Greenough).

*124. ————. <u>Novellas exemplares: or, exemplary novels, in six books</u>.
Printed for C. Hitch, S. Birt, J. Brindley, etc. 396pp. 12mo. 3s. (H; I; N)

Each of the six novels has an individual title page dated 1742.

This translation, by Thomas Shelton, was first published c.1615.

Translated from <u>Novelas exemplares</u>, 1613.

a. 1746. _Instructive and entertaining novels; designed to promote virtue, good sense, and universal benevolence._ Printed for J. Nourse. 396pp. 12mo. 3_s_. (H; I; N; Y)

A re-issue of _Novellas exemplares_, with a new master title-page.

b. 1747. _Instructive and entertaining novels . . ._ . Dublin: Printed for William Brien, R. James, and W. Ransom. 314pp. 12mo. (BM)

This collection includes only the six love stories from the _Novelas exemplares_.

125. Fénelon, François de Salignac de la Mothe. _The adventures of Telemachus, the son of Ulysses_. Printed for J. Walthoe and T. Waller. 2 vols. 12mo. 6_s_. (H; LC)

Translated by John Kelly, Esq.

See also above, Nos. 28 and 103, and below, No. 126.

126. ————. _The first four books of Telemachus_. Newcastle. 57pp. 12mo. (Y)

Extracted and translated by Henry Swinhoe.

See also above, Nos. 28, 103, and 125.

*127. Gomez, Madeleine Angélique Poisson de. La belle assemblée: or, the adventures of six days.
Fifth edition. Printed for D. Browne, etc. 4 vols. 12mo.
(BPL)

This translation, by Eliza Haywood, was first published in 1724 (Whicher).

Translated from Les journées amusantes, Vols. I-IV, 1722-1724.
(McBurney No. 167.)

a. 1749. Sixth edition. Printed for D. Browne, J. Brotherton, W. Meadows, etc. 4 vols. 12mo. (Bro)

An "assembly" collection of eighteen novels told by the members of a company to amuse and edify each other during their stay at a country house. The framework also includes conversations on love, morals, politics, and so on. Many of the tales imitate Boccaccio, Cervantes' exemplary novels, or Mme. de La Fayette's nouvelles.

*128. Gueulette, Thomas Simon. Mogul tales, or, the dreams of men awake: being stories told to divert the sultana's of Guzurat, for the supposed death of the sultan.
Second edition. Printed for J. Brindley, J. Wilcox, J. Hodges, etc. 2 vols. 12mo. (I; P)

This translation was first published in 1736 (McBurney No. 316).

Translated from Les sultanes de Guzarate, ou les songes des hommes éveillés, contes moguls, 1732.

Like the same author's Chinese tales (see above, No. 29) and Peruvian tales (see below, No. 278), this is a pseudo-oriental imitation of the Arabian nights (see below, No. 179).

129. Marivaux, Pierre de Carlet de Chamblain. The virtuous orphan: or, the life of Marianne.
4 vols. 8vo. (H; Y)

Freely translated by Mary Collyer from La vie de Marianne, 1731-1741.

See also above, No. 77 (the original translation), and below, No. 212.

a. 1747. Second edition. Printed for J. Robinson.
2 vols. 12mo. 6s. (BM)

130. Prévost d'Exiles, Antoine François, Abbé. The memoirs and adventures of the Marquis de Bretagne and Duc d'Harcourt.

Printed for T. Cooper. 3 vols. 12mo. 9s. (C; H)

A strangely titled new translation, by William Erskine, of *Mémoires d'un homme de qualité*, 1728-1731.

See also above, No. 80, for the original translation.

a. 1745. (Foster).

*131. Tyssot de Patot, Simon. *The travels and adventures of James Massey*.

Second edition: Printed for J. Watts. 370pp. 12mo. (I; N)

This translation, by Stephen Whatley, was first published in 1732 (McBurney No. 287).

Translated from *Voyages et avantures de Jaques Massé*, 1710.

An imaginary voyage combining the adventures of shipwreck and combat at sea with the satirical purpose of a visit to a utopian paradise where religious Quietism and a benevolent monarchy prevail.

1744

See also above, Nos. 26, 46, 47, 49, 77, 80, 81, 84, 99, 105, 118, 121, and 123, and below, No. 278.

132. Clidanor and Cecilia. A novel.

Printed for M. Cooper. 87pp. 8vo. 1s. (Chi)

A pious domestic novel about the love and virtues of the titular characters, whose story is "adapted to form the Mind to a just Way of Thinking, and to a proper Manner of behaving in Life."

133. The fair adultress: or, the treacherous brother. Being the secret memoirs of a certain noble family in the island of Cyprus.

Printed for A. Millar and J. Perry. 48pp. 8vo. 2s. (BM)

A brief novel of scandal in high life.

134. The fair German, or the amours of Theresa.

Printed for W. Bickerton. 58pp. 8vo. 1s. (N)

This story of the first nineteen years in the life of a roguish prostitute claims to be a translation from the French, but is actually a slander of Mrs. Teresia Constantia Phillips, a notorious lady whose reputation was finally defended in a fictionalized Apology (1748-1749: below, No. 237).

135. Fortune's favourite: containing, memoirs of the many hardships and sufferings, together with the surprizing deliverance and advancement to plenty and happiness, of Jacobo Anglicano, a young nobleman.
Printed for the author. 384pp. 12mo. (N)

A plagiarism of the first two parts of James Annesley's Memoirs of an unfortunate young nobleman (1743: above, No. 113).

136. The lady's drawing room. Being a faithful picture of the great world.
Printed for M. Cooper. 329pp. 12mo. 3s. (C; H; P)

a. 1746. Dublin: Printed for George and Alexander Ewing. 12mo. (BM)

b. 1748. Second edition. Printed for A. Millar. 329pp. 12mo. (I; N)

An "assembly" collection of brief amorous novels, imaginary voyages, and moral _histoires_, told to each other by the daily visitors to the drawing room of the beautiful Ethelinda, who has banished cards and gossip in favor of the edifying art of storytelling.

137. _Leisure hours amusements. Being a select collection of one hundred and fifty of the most humorous and diverting stories_.
Printed for M. Cooper. 318pp. 12mo. (N)

A collection of very brief novels and _histoires_, which also includes stories and tales digested from the _Spectator_ and _Tatler_ papers.

*138. _Letters from a Persian in England to his friend at Ispahan_.
Fifth edition. Printed for J. Millan. 324pp. 12mo. (I; N)
First published in 1735 as _The Persian letters continued: or, the second volume of letters from Selim at London, to Mirza at Ispahan_ (McBurney No. 297).

This spurious continuation of George Lyttleton's anti-Walpole satirical "spy" fiction _Letters from a Persian in England_ (1735: McBurney No. 299) makes the same arguments against the Whig oligarchy, but from a Jacobite's point of view. The first half of the mini-heroic romance _Celenia and Adrastes_ (see above, No. 87) is interwoven.

139. _The progress of nature, exemplify'd in the life of Roger Lovejoy, Esq_.
Printed for T. Wiltshire. 95pp. 8vo. 1_s_. (Y)

A fictional biography of an alleged Methodist preacher, whose life has been constantly burdened by the knowledge of his illegitimate birth as the son of a reprobate Anglican prelate.

140. _The remarkable case of William Bower, of York, convicted for the robbery of Mr. Levit Harris_.
Printed for Jackson and Dodd. 110pp. 8vo. 1_s_. (BM)

A sensational account of the escapades of a notorious robber, together with a summary of his trial and some "new revelations" about his crimes.

141. The second court secret; a moving scene for the year seventeen hundred forty-three, interspersed with a remarkable fragment of secret history.
Printed for J. Brown. 47pp. 8vo. (P)

An imitation of George Lyttleton's scathing orientalized satire of Sir Robert Walpole, The court secret (1741: above, No. 61).

142. Thelamont; or, perfect generosity. A novel.
Printed for M. Cooper. 113pp. 12mo. 1s. (BM)

A routine sentimental novel about virtuous love and its rewards.

143. The true history of the life and sudden death of old John Overs.
Printed for T. Harris. 30pp. 4to. 6d. (H)

An exaggerated tale of how an old rich ferry-man was consumed by his greed, which killed him and grieved his daughter, who donated her inherited riches to the Church. St. Mary Overs in Southwark, the narrative tells us, was built as a consequence of her pious giving.

144. A woeful voyage indeed: being a full and particular account of the voyage, adventures, and distresses of the crew belonging to the nimble Nancy.
8vo. (BM)

A brief voyage narrative attacking incompetence in the English Navy, and describing a "dangerous" voyage to the Nore.

145. Bishop, Matthew. The life and adventures of Matthew Bishop. Giving an account of several engagements he was concern'd in.
Printed for J. Brindley. 283pp. 8vo. 4s. (H)

A fictionalized autobiography of one of Marlborough's lowliest foot-soldiers who distorts historical events to inflate his own importance and who, by his own claim, was never "intimidated as most Men are" by the sight of ever so many enemies, but rather "always animated."

146. Collyer, Mary. Felicia to Charlotte: being letters from a young lady in the country, to her friend in town, Vol. I.
Printed for J. Robinson. 310pp. 12mo. 3s. (BM)

a. 1749. Third edition of Vol. I, together with the new "Volume Second." Printed for R. Griffiths and G. Woodfall (Vol. I), and for J. Payne and J. Bouquet (Vol. II). 2 vols. 12mo. (H; N; P; Y; Chi; Duk)

Mrs. Collyer's comic love story borrows its ironic spirit from Cervantes and Fielding, its epistolary method from Marivaux (whom the authoress translated) and Richardson.

*147. Davys, Mary. The reform'd coquet: or, memoirs of Amoranda. A novel.

Fifth edition. 154pp. 12mo. (N)

First published in 1724 (McBurney No. 154).

A domestic love comedy telling the story of a sprightly, wealthy orphan girl named Amoranda, whose innocent coquetry gets her into difficulties, but whose virtue ensures that she will be rewarded with happiness in marriage to a virtuous youth who has all along been with her, disguised as her aged Mentor Formator.

*148. Defoe, Daniel. The whole life and strange surprizing adventures of Robinson Crusoe of York, mariner.

Dublin: Printed for G. Golding and I. Jackson, 1744-1745. 2 vols. 12mo. (Leh)

Includes _The farther adventures of Robinson Crusoe_.

Both works were first published in 1719, under the titles _The life and strange surprizing adventures of Robinson Crusoe_, and _The farther adventures . . ._ (Moore). (McBurney Nos. 99 and 98, respectively.)

a. 1740. Eighth edition of _Crusoe_, together with the sixth edition of _The farther adventures_. 2 vols. 12mo. (Advertised by Osborn in _Chinese tales_, 1740.)

A re-issue from 1736 (BM).

b. 1747. Ninth edition of _Crusoe_, together with the seventh edition of _The farther adventures_. Printed for T. Woodward. 2 vols. 12mo. (I; Y)

c. 1748. Another edition of _Crusoe_. 12mo. (Greenough).

149. Fielding, Sarah. _The adventures of David Simple_. Printed for A. Millar. 2 vols. 12mo. 6_s_. (I; N; P)

a. 1744. Second edition. Printed for A. Millar. 2 vols. 12mo. (I; P)

This edition includes an important Preface by Henry Fielding, who also revised and corrected the text.

Miss Fielding's story of her virtuous quixotic hero's journey through London and Westminster "in search of a Friend" tries to fuse Richardson's sentiment and Henry Fielding's wit and irony, but is best described as moral allegory. A third volume, "in which this History is concluded," appeared in 1753.

150. Haywood, Eliza. <u>The fortunate foundlings: being the genuine history of Colonel M——rs, and his sister, Madam du P——y</u>.
Printed for T. Gardner. 352pp. 12mo. 3<u>s</u>. (H; I; N)

a. 1745. Dublin. 12mo. (H; P)

b. 174[?]. Second edition [?]. (Whicher).

c. 1748. Third edition. Printed for T. Gardner. 331pp. 12mo. 3<u>s</u>. (I; Y)

The story of the foundling twins Louisa and Horatio, born in the year 1688 and subjected to all manner of testing before receiving the rewards of station, fortune, and marital bliss to which their virtues entitle them. Louisa recalls Richardson's Pamela, while the martial Horatio resembles Defoe's military heroes. Mrs. Haywood's success with a dual plot anticipates the achievement of Fielding's Tom Jones (1749: below, No. 272).

*151. Lucas, Theophilus. Authentic memoirs of the lives, intrigues, and comical adventures of the most eminent gamesters and celebrated sharpers.
Printed for the editor. 147pp. 12mo. 1s. (BM)
First published in 1714 (McBurney No. 71).

A collection of short narrative accounts of the deceits and swindles practiced by gamblers and sharpers of all kinds against young men too free with their money. Offered as a "warning" to the unwary.

152. Pearsall, Richard, Rev. The power and pleasure of the divine life: exemplify'd in the late Mrs. Housman.
12mo. (BM)

This widely reprinted narrative fictionalizes the genuine life of a persecuted, exemplary lady, whose pious martyrdom ended in a "triumphant" death.

153. Smith, William, Esq. <u>A new voyage to Guinea</u>. Printed for J. Nourse. 176pp. 8vo. 4<u>s</u>. (P)

A mildly sensational, strongly partisan narrative account of a voyage to the Guinea settlements, and of the climate, customs, manners, and so on that may be found there. Smith was a member of the Royal African Company, whose directors commissioned this book.

TRANSLATIONS

154. <u>A select collection of singular and interesting histories. . . . Translated from the original French</u>. Printed for A. Millar. 2 vols. 12mo. 6<u>s</u>. (H)

A collection of sensational accounts of Continental robbers and murderers, together with summaries of their trials and, in some cases, records of their executions.

155. Gomez, Madeleine Angélique Poisson de. <u>The memoirs of the Baron Du Tan. To which is added The Calabrian: or, the history of Charles Brachy, and the hermit</u>. Printed for H. Piers, M. Wentz, and M. Cooper. 278pp. 8vo. 3<u>s</u>. (H; N)

Extracted and translated from _Les cent nouvelles nouvelles_, 1732-1739.

See also below, No. 180.

A collection of three brief novels: one is a sentimental memoir of domestic intrigue in a baron's family; the second is an imaginary voyage incorporating a pseudo-oriental setting and telling a sentimental love story involving Algerian slavery and heroic rescues; the third is the melancholy tale of a hermit driven into solitude by the supposed treachery of his brother and the consequent death of his beloved wife.

156. La Fontaine, Jean de. _The loves of Cupid and Psyche; in verse and prose . . . with a new life of La Fontaine_. Printed for H. Chapelle. 368pp. 4to. (N; LC)

Translated by John Lockman from _Amours de Psyché et de Cupidon_ (1669).

1745

See also above, Nos. 18, 32, 65, 72, 120, 130, and 150, and below, No. 278.

157. The adventures of a night; or, the island of absurdities.

Printed for J. Collyer. 27pp. 8vo. 6d. (H; Y)

A satire of George II and the conduct of the War of Jenkins' Ear, in the form of an imitation of the satirical "Night adventurer" segment of Quevedo's Visions (re-issued 1745: below, No. 188).

158. The agreeable companion; or, an universal medley of wit and good-humour.

Printed for W. Bickerton. 383pp. 8vo. (N; Y)

A miscellaneous collection of essays, epigrams, satirical poems, dialogues, and very brief exemplary novels.

159. The compendious library: or, pocket companion for winter evening entertainments.

Printed for G. Smith. 288pp. 12mo. 3s. (I)

A collection containing fictionalized "narratives of the most remarkable revolutions, conquests, and insurrections," along with "historical accounts of several foreign countries, and of such things as are therein most worthy of observance."

160. The fortunate orphan: or, memoirs of the Countess of Marlou.
242pp. 12mo. 2s.6d. (N)

An anonymous native imitation of the Chevalier de Mouhy's La paysanne parvenue, 1735-1737. For two other versions of the same story, see above, Nos. 30 and 107.

161. The history of Polly Willis. An orphan.
Printed by W. Reeve. 243pp. 12mo. (P)

A domestic novel about a virtuous young orphan girl who, after many affecting troubles, has her goodness rewarded by happy marriage to a wealthy suitor, the good Mr. Warren. The story resembles Richardson's Pamela (1740: above, No. 23), although it is a straightforward third-person narrative.

162. Leonora; or, characters drawn from real life. Printed for Thomas Davies. 2 vols. 12mo. (N; P)

a. 1745. Second edition. Printed for T. Davies. 2 vols. 12mo. (H)

An intensely didactic novel focusing on the loves of the pious heroine Leonora, but also displaying the innocuous romantic adventures of stereotyped characters with names like Fidelia, Horatius, Camilla, and Hypolitus.

*163. The lover's secretary; or, the adventures of Lindamira, a lady of quality. Written to her friend in the country. In XXIV letters. Revis'd and corrected by Mr. Tho. Brown. Fifth edition. Dublin: Printed for Joseph Rhames. 160pp. 8vo. (N; Bro)

First published in 1702 as The adventures of Lindamira, a lady of quality . . . (McBurney No. 7).

This is one of the most famous and important of early epistolary novels written in English. As a domestic love story, it also anticipated Richardson's Pamela (1740: above, No. 23).

164. Polite amusements, containing select histories equally instructive and entertaining.
Printed for M. Cooper. 362pp. 12mo. 2s.6d. (H)

A collection of three sentimental novels of extremely tender passion, allegedly translated from the French but obviously by an English imitator of Mrs. Eliza Haywood's early novels of amorous intrigue.

165. Popish intrigues and cruelty plainly exemplified, in the affecting case and narrative of Mrs. Francis Shaftoe.
Second edition. Printed for M. Cooper. 24pp. 8vo. (BM)
No first edition known.

A sensational anti-Catholic story of a virtuous lady lodging with the family of the Popish "Sir Theophilus Oglethorpe," where she overhears many treasonable conversations, is tricked into a journey to France, and barbarously used in order to make her a nun.

166. "Gorion, Abraham Ben." The book of the chronicles of the chief minister of E——d. Translated from the original Arabic of Abraham Ben Gorion: a descendant of the historian Josephus. In two books.

"Printed for Zimri, the son of Korah." 12pp. folio. (N)

A curious satire of Sir Robert Walpole, published three years after the Prime Minister's fall from power. The format resembles the biblical Chronicle; the "Books," "Chapters," and "verses" purport to account sequentially for the "Minister's" career.

167. Carew, Bampfylde-Moore. _The life and adventures of Bampfylde-Moore-Carew, the noted Devonshire stroller and dog-stealer. As related by himself, during his passage to the plantations in America_.
Printed for Joseph Drew. 152pp. 5to. 2_s_. (BM)
See also below, No. 271.

a. 1745. _The accomplished vagabond; or the compleat mumper_. (_NCBEL_).
Another issue of _The life and adventures_, with a new title.

The famous quasi-autobiographical narrative of the spirited mendicant gypsy whom many contemporary readers apparently identified with the gypsy king featured by Fielding in Book XII of _Tom Jones_ (1749: below, No. 272).

*168. Defoe, Daniel. <u>Memoirs of a cavalier</u>.
Leeds: Printed for James Lister, [c.1745-1750]. 338pp. 8vo.
(I)

First published in 1720 (McBurney No. 113).

169. Drummond, John. <u>The affecting case, and dying words of Mr. Arch[ibald]. Oswald, an ensign in the young Pretender's service</u>.
Printed for J. Robinson. 32pp. 8vo. 6d. (H)

A romanticized account of the heroic service and tragic fall of a brave young soldier who died of three musket shots at the Battle of Preston-Pans.

170. Green, John, ed. <u>A new general collection of voyages and travels</u>.
Printed for Thomas Astley. 4 vols. 4to. (Y)

These four massive volumes include all kinds of voyages: some are unquestionably authentic, others are on the borderlines of fiction, and a great many are fabrications. One of the longest narratives included is Daniel Defoe's <u>The four years voyages of Captain George Roberts</u>, first published in 1726 (Moore; McBurney No. 192).

171. Kirkby, John. The capacity and extent of the human understanding; exemplified in the extraordinary case of Automathes; a young nobleman.
Printed for R. Manby and H. Shute Cox. 248pp. 12mo. 3s.
(H; N; P; Y)

a. 1746. Second edition. Dublin: Printed for George Faulkner. 228pp. 12mo. (P)

b. 1747. Second edition. Printed for R. Manby and H. Shute Cox. 248pp. 12mo. (C)

A padded plagiarism of The history of Autonous (1736: McBurney No. 308), Automathes combines Crusoesque desert-island adventure and utopian polemics. It tells the story of a youth who, lost and alone on an island from infancy until maturity, deduces all Christian knowledge from his natural surroundings and grows up into a young Anglican gentleman, thus exemplifying the principles of natural theology.

172. McCarthy, Charlotte. The fair moralist: or, love and virtue.
Printed for R. Baldwin. 220pp. 12mo. 1s.6d. (BM)

a. 1745. 12mo. (BM)

b. 1746. Second edition. Printed for B. Stichall and R. Baldwin. 220pp. 12mo. (N; P)

A sentimental novel about a virtuous young heroine named Emelia. Resolute resistance to temptation and lewd advances finally win Emelia the love of her persecutor, whom she rejects, however, in favor of a more worthy husband. The resemblances to Richardson's Pamela (1740: above, No. 23) are many and obvious.

173. Nelson, John. The case of John Nelson, written by himself.
Second edition. Printed for T. Trye. 32pp. 12mo. 3d. (BM)

No first edition known.

An impassioned autobiographical account of a Yorkshire stone-mason's dramatic conversion by one of John Wesley's sermons, and of his subsequent career as a Methodist preacher. This pious narrative was rather widely reprinted throughout the eighteenth and early nineteenth centuries.

174. Thompson, R. _The Atalantis reviv'd: being, a select collection of novels, of illustrious persons of both sexes_. Printed for C. Corbet, 1745-1748. 2 vols. 12mo. (N: Vol. II only; BM)

The title page of Vol. II is dated 1748, and bears the title _The young ladies and gentlemens amorous amusement . . . . Or, the Atalantis reviv'd_.

An alleged imitation of Mrs. Manley's _New Atalantis_ (1709: McBurney No. 45); includes innocuous accounts of such real people as Margaret of Parma and the Duchess of Mazarine, interspersed with brief amorous novels.

TRANSLATIONS

175. _The Perseis, or secret memoirs for a history of Persia_.
Printed for J. Roberts. 220pp. 12mo. 2_s_. (BM)

Translated from _Mémoires secrets pour servir à l'histoire de Perse_ (Amsterdam, 1745).

For another translation of this work see below, No. 176.

A pseudo-oriental political satire presenting a series of scandalous anecdotes about the politics and royal Courts of the principal nations of Europe, all tied together by a thinly disguised narrative record of the life of Louis XV of France.

176. The secret history of Persia. Containing a particular account, not only of that kingdom, but also of the most considerable states of Asia.
Printed for M. Cooper. 220pp. 12mo. 3s. (H)
Translated from Mémoires secrets pour servir à l'histoire de Perse (Amsterdam, 1745).
For another translation of this work see above, No. 175.

177. "Isabella, Lady Donna." Iberian tales and novels. Translated from the Spanish originals.
Printed for E. Curll. 394pp. 12mo. 4s. (BM)

A collection of exemplary novels in imitation of Cervantes and Alonzo de Castillo.

178. Caylus, Anne Claude Philippe, comte de. Oriental tales, collected from an Arabian manuscript, in the library of the King of France.

Printed for T. Trye, W. Shropshire, and M. Cooper. 2 vols. 4to. 5*s*. (N; Y; UCLA)

Translated from *Contes orienteaux, tirés des manuscrits de la bibliotheque du roy de France* (The Hague, 1743).

a. 1749. Printed for T. Trye. 2 vols. 6*s*. (Listed in *GM* May 1749).

A parody of the many collections of oriental tales by Thomas Simon Gueulette (see above, No. 29) and others. The frame-tale presents Moradbak, whose task is to tell soporific tales that will alleviate the insomnia of Hudjadge, King of Persia. She succeeds so well that, as a reward, he makes her his Queen.

179. Galland, Antoine. *Arabian nights entertainments, consisting of one thousand and one stories, told by the sultaness of the Indies to divert the sultan.* 1745-1748. 12 vols. in 6. 8vo. (BM)

This is a new translation of *Les mille et une nuits, contes arabes*, 1704-1717.

See also below, No. A19.

(For the original publication of the first English translation of 1706-1717, see McBurney No. 23.)

180. Gomez, Madeleine Angélique Poisson de. Select novels, translated from the French.
Printed for T. Gardner and W. Shropshire. 336pp. 12mo. 3s. (H; I; P)
Translated from Les cent nouvelles nouvelles, 1732-1739.

One of several gatherings of tales translated from Mme. de Gomez's popular collection of original nouvelles (see also above, No. 155), virtually all of which are sentimental stories of tender passion, whether set at the domestic hearthside or in the mysterious East.

181. Le Sage, Alain, René. The adventures of Robert Chevalier, call'd De Beauchene. Captain of a privateer in New-France.
Printed for T. Gardner, R. Dodsley, and M. Cooper. 2 vols. 12mo. 6s. (H; N; Y; LC)
Translated from Les avantures de Monsieur Robert Chevalier, dit de Beauchêne, 1732.

A picaresque narrative about a pirate whose life and adventures bear some striking resemblances to Defoe's Captain Singleton, 1720 (Moore; McBurney No. 112).

182. ———. Henry and Blanche; or, the revengeful marriage.

Printed for R. Dodsley. 67pp. 4to. 2s. (P; Y)

A comic tale of love and intrigue extracted from the author's famous Gil Blas, 1715-1735 (see above, No. 105).

183. ———. The history of the life and adventures of the famous knight, Don Quixote, by "Alfonso Fernandez de Avellaneda."

Printed for Paul Vaillant. 2 vols. 12mo. 6s. (I)

Translated by Mr. Baker from Nouvelles aventures de l'admirable don Quichotte, 1704, which was adapted from Felipe Roberto de Tarragona's La segunda parte del ingenioso hidalgo D. Quijote de la Mancha, 1614. (For the original English translation from Le Sage, see McBurney No. 19.)

A spurious continuation of Cervantes' Don Quixote (see above, No. 27).

184. Mouhy, Charles de Fieux, Chevalier de. Injur'd innocence; being the instructive and diverting memoirs of the Marquis de Fieux.

Printed for Meadows. 2 vols. in 1. 12mo. (Y)

Translated from _Mémoires de Monsieur le marquix de Fieux_, 1735-1736.

These alleged "memoirs" actually take the form of a sentimental novel depicting the unwarranted suffering, and final rewards of love and fortune, of a virtuous young gentleman.

*185. Palafox y Mendoza, Juan de. _The new odyssey, by the Spanish Homer; being the travels of the Christian hero, Ulysses Desiderius Pius_.

Dublin: Printed for Ignatius Kelly. 160pp. 12mo. (I)

This translation was first published in London, 1735 (N).

Translated from _El Pastor de noche buena_, 1659.

(McBurney No. X41.)

A passionate Bunyanesque spiritual allegory of personal salvation, written by the famous seventeenth-century Spanish Quietist. Fénelon acknowledged this work as one of the models for his didactic romance of _Télémaque_, 1699-1700 (see above, No. 28).

*186. Pöllnitz, Karl Ludwig, Freiherr von. Les amusemens de spa: or the gallantries of the spaw in Germany.
Third edition. Printed for S. Birt and W. Sandby. 2 vols. 12mo. 5s.6d. (H; P)

This translation was first published in 1737 (McBurney No. 325).

Translated by Hans de Veil from Amusemens des eaux de spa (Amsterdam, 1734).

Secret histories of the amours and intrigues of Continental high life, set against the background of a fashionable German watering-place.

187. Quevedo y Villegas, Francisco Gomez de. The comical works of Don Francisco de Quevedo.
Printed for the translator. 8vo. (BM)

A new translation by Peter Pineda.

See also above, No. 109.

a. 1743. 8vo. (Greenough).

*188. ———. The visions of Dom Francisco de Quevedo Villegas.
Printed for J. Collyer. 220pp. 12mo. (H; I)

This translation, by Sir Roger L'Estrange, was first published in 1667 (BM).

Translated from Sueños y discursos de verdades, 1667.

Terse satirical sketches, narrated in the form of dreams or visions, by the author of the famous picaresque romance El buscón, 1626 (see above, No. 109).

*189. Ramsay, Andrew. The travels of Cyrus. Seventh edition. Printed for C. Hitch. 358pp. 12mo. (BM)

This translation, by Nathaniel Hooke, was first published in 1727 (McBurney No. 222).

Translated from Voyages de Cyrus, 1727.

A popular imitation of Fénelon's famous didactic romance of Télémaque (see above, No. 28); adapted from Xenophon by the French-speaking Scot who served as tutor to the Stuart Pretender's children.

1746

See also above, Nos. 26, 65, 84, 104, 105, 124, 136, 171, and 172.

190. *A compleat history of the intrigues of priests and nuns.*
Printed for Richard Adams. 311pp. 12mo. (BM)

Brief, lewd narratives of amorous scandals in convents and churches. Maliciously anti-Catholic and anti-Jacobite.

191. *Genuine memoirs of the life of Simon Lord Fraser of Lovat.*
Printed for M. Cooper. 57pp. 8vo. (H)

This brief account of the famous Scottish eccentric stretches truth in support of its anti-Jacobite argument, although it is mildly sympathetic to Fraser himself.

192. *A journey to Llandrindod Wells, in Radnorshire . . . and to which is prefix'd . . . a poem, by way of apology for the author's writing. By a countryman.*
Birmingham: Printed for B. Haslewood. 84pp. 8vo. 1*s*. (Y)

A jocose, satirical account of a journey to Wales, deliberately and ironically written in crude colloquial English by a mocking "Countryman."

193. *The life of Cassem, the son of Hamid, a noble Arabian. Translated from an oriental manuscript.* Printed for James Buckland. 48pp. 4to. 1*s*. (Chi)

An account of an imaginary Eastern prophet whose noble bearing, solitary life, and brilliant mind all make him an exceptional being, and whose "profound" philosophical and theological speculations make him sound like an apologist for Low Church Anglicanism.

194. *Memoirs of Mr. George Fane, a London merchant. Who suffered three years of slavery in the country of Algiers.* 20pp. 8vo. (Y)

a. 1746. Included in *Beau's miscellany* (below, No. 199).

b. 1748. 20pp. 8vo. (Greenough).

A sensational story of a pleasant young middle-class rogue whose affair with a Duke's illegitimate daughter causes his exile and slavery, but whose adventures end with his return, marriage to the lady, and consequent gain of an estate worth 6,000 pounds per year.

195. Memoirs of the lives and families of the Lords Kilmarnock, Cromarty, and Balmorins.
Printed for T. Gardner. 52pp. 8vo. 1s. (Y)
See also below, No. 213.

a. 1746. Third edition. 64pp. 8vo. (Y)

Sensational, fictionalized biographical sketches of three Jacobites tried and executed for the support they gave Prince Charles Edward Stuart during the "'forty-five."

196. Philamour and Philamena: or genuine memoirs of a late affecting transaction.
Printed for T. Gardner. 72pp. 4to. 1s. (N)

A mildly sensational tale of the almost unrelieved misery of a girl named Philamena whose happiness is ruined by an arranged marriage, which leads to an illicit affair, and finally to her brutal murder at the hands of her own son.

197. The travels of Tom Thumb over England and Wales. Printed for Amey. 144pp. 12mo. 1s.6d. (N)

Having escaped from the cow's belly, the little folk hero now provides a narrative record of his domestic travels.

198. "Biron, Felicité de." The adventures and amours of the Marquis de Noailles, and Mademoiselle Tencin. Printed for J. Robinson. 2 vols. 12mo. (P)

A sentimental novel, with undertones of the chronique scandaleuse, about a rich and virtuous nobleman's strife to hurdle the romantic and social obstacles blocking his marriage to an impeccable but common heroine.

199. "Broadbottom, Bartholomew." Beau's miscellany; or, the agreeable variety in prose and verse. Printed by David Simple, for Joseph Andrews and sold by Abraham Adams. Printed for E. Boyd, 1746[?]. 276pp. 8vo. (N; Y)

A collection of tales, histories, and poems; includes a reprint of the roguish Memoirs of Mr. George Fane, a London merchant (1746: above, No. 194).

200. Arbuthnot, Archibald. The life, adventures, and many great vicissitudes of fortune of Simon, Lord Lovat, the head of the family of Frasers.

Printed for R. Walker. 280pp. 8vo. (N; P)

See also below, No. 215.

a. 1746. 305pp. 8vo. (BM)

b. 1748. Printed for R. Walker. 8vo. (Greenough).

The most extensive contemporary account of the famous Scottish Jacobite, who was executed for support given to Prince Charles Edward Stuart. Although based on facts, Arbuthnot's book fictionalizes Lovat's life by stretching his eccentricities and making him a buffoon, all in the interest of the author's anti-Jacobite polemical purpose.

201. ———. Memoirs of the remarkable life and surprizing adventures of Miss Jenny Cameron.

Printed for R. Walker. 280pp. 4to. (N; UCLA)

a. 1746. A brief account of the life and family of Miss Jenny Cameron.

Printed for T. Gardner. 47pp. 8vo. (I; Ind)

A condensed version of Arbuthnot's original.

b. 1746. Dublin: Printed for W. Brien. 72pp. 12mo. (I) Another condensation.

An anti-Jacobite's lively fictionalized account of the roguish girl who, in her mid-forties, became the mistress of Prince Charles Edward Stuart, and accompanied him during the "'forty-five."

202. Burton, John. Ascanius, or, the young adventurer; a true history.
Printed for T. Johnston. 288pp. 12mo. 2s.6d. (P)

a. 1746. Printed for Smith. 1s. (Listed in GM Dec. 1746).

b. 1747. Printed for the proprietor. 288pp. 8vo. (H; Y)

A romanticized, rather unsympathetic treatment of the life, adventures, and crimes of Prince Charles Edward Stuart, with particular emphasis on the "'forty-five." According to P. J. Anderson, this was probably the most popular of all the narratives on this glamorous subject: see N&Q, Twelfth Ser., 12 (Jan.-June 1923), 172.

203. F., A. <u>The general entertainer: or, a collection of near three hundred polite tales and fables</u>.
Printed for H. Slater and R. Adams. 2 vols. 12mo. (BM)

Inflated, romanticized "lives" of the "Greatest Persons . . . in the World."

204. Fielding, Henry. <u>The female husband; or, the surprizing history of Mrs. Mary, alias Mr George Hamilton</u>.
Printed for T. Cooper. 23pp. 8vo. 6<u>d</u>. (Hun)

A piece of sensational journalism dealing with the exploits of a roguish vixen convicted of duping and marrying another young woman. According to Sheridan Baker, the pamphlet was patched together from court records and newspaper accounts by a Fielding desperate for money.

205. Forbes, Duncan [?]. <u>Memoirs of the life of the Lord Lovat</u>.
Printed for M. Cooper. 123pp. 8vo. 1<u>s</u>.6<u>d</u>. (Y)

a. 1747. Third edition. Dublin: Printed for W. Brien. 71pp. 8vo. (Y)

A fictionalized biography of the famous Scottish Jacobite who was executed for his support of Prince Charles Edward Stuart in the "'forty-five."

206. Foster, James. An account of the behaviour of the late Earl of Kilmarnock, after his sentence and on the day of his execution.
Dublin: Printed for George Faulkner, Oliver Nelson, W. Bryen, etc. 43pp. 4to. (H)

A narrative of the author's alleged conversations with the Jacobite Earl just before his execution for treason, and of how the criminal was brought by Foster's eloquence to look rightly upon the blackness of his public and private crimes, thus saving his soul.

207. L., H. The leak in the vessel: or, Captain Meanwell's adventures.
Printed for M. Cooper. 42pp. 8vo. (N)

A chapbook moral allegory in which a narrator describes how he navigated the "vessel" of his soul from a sea of spiritual turmoil and darkness, into the safe harbor of faith. The volume includes also an account of trade with Spain, and a brief life of William III of England.

*208. Longueville, Peter. *The hermit: or, the unparalled [sic] sufferings and surprising adventures of Mr. Philip Quarll, an Englishman*.
Printed for J. Osborn. 264pp. 8vo. 2*s*.6*d*. (N)
First published in 1727 (McBurney No. 216).

a. 1742. *The history and surprizing adventures of Mr. Philip Quarll, the English hermit*. (Greenough).

b. 1748. (Listed in *LM* April-May 1748).

A very popular imitation of *Robinson Crusoe* (see above, No. 148), although Longueville's hero is less resourceful than Defoe's, and even more dependent on Providence.

209. Macdonald, Allan, or George Granville, Baron Lansdowne. *Alexis, or the young adventurer. A novel*.
Edinburgh: Printed for A. Scott. 15pp. 4to. (H; I)

a. 1746. Printed for T. Cooper. 30pp. 8vo. (H; N; P)

The story of the Young Pretender's frightening adventures after the Battle of Culloden Moor.

*210. Swift, Jonathan. The works of Jonathan Swift. Dublin: Printed for G. Faulkner. 8 vols. 12mo. (P)

a. 1747. Sixth edition. Dublin: Printed for G. Faulkner. 9 vols. 12mo. (P; I: 8 vols. only)

This particular collection of Swift's complete Works, apparently the first of two published by George Faulkner, was originally issued in 1735 (Teerink).

TRANSLATIONS

*211. Claude, Isaac. The amours of the Count de Soissons, a Prince of the House of Bourbon.
224pp. 8vo. (BM)

This translation, by James Seguin, was first published in 1729 (McBurney No. 244).

Translated from Le Comte de Soissons, nouvelle galante, 1687.

Secret histories of the gallantries of "Persons of Distinction" at the French Court during the days of Cardinal Richelieu.

212. Marivaux, Pierre de Carlet de Chamblain. _The life and adventures of Indiana, the virtuous orphan_.
Printed for C. Whitefield. 453pp. 8vo. (I; P; Y)

An adaptation of Mary Collyer's _Virtuous orphan_ (1743: above, No. 129), an earlier free translation of _La vie de Marianne_, 1731-1741.

See also above, No. 77, for the original English translation.

1747

See also above, Nos. 10, 25, 27, 53, 66, 90, 97, 100, 113, 117, 124, 129, 148, 171, 202, 205, and 210.

213. _An account of the apparition of the late Lord Kilmarnock to the Rev^{d} Mr. Foster . . . . To which is added, the second appearing of the late Lord Kilmarnock, to a clergyman of the Church of England_.
Printed for M. Cooper. 29pp. 8vo. (H)

Two short "reports" of the allegedly resurrected rebel's conversations with two men of the cloth. Another anti-Jacobite treatment of the Scottish laird's role in the "'forty-five," for which he was executed in 1746 (see also above, No. 195).

214. _Adventures of a kidnapped orphan_.

Printed for M. Thrush. 252pp. 12mo. (H; P)

A narrative account of the fortunes and misfortunes of an impeccably virtuous, courageous orphan named Thomas Page, who was impressed aboard an Indiaman, and plunged into mercurial adventures ending with his melancholy death in Calcutta. In some of its pictures of shipboard life and characters, this work forecasts Smollett's _Roderick Random_ (1748: below, No. 253).

215. _A candid and impartial account of the behaviour of Simon Lord Lovat, from the time his death-warrant was deliver'd, to the day of his execution . . . by a gentleman who attended his lordship in his last moments_.

Printed for J. Newbery and W. Faden. 29pp. 4to. (H)

Romanticized treatment of the most famous of the Scottish Jacobites, who had been given fuller and more judicious attention in Archibald Arbuthnot's _The life, adventures, and many and great vicissitudes . . . of Simon, Lord Lovat_ (1746: above, No. 200).

216. The female rebels: being some remarkable incidents of the lives, characters, and families of the titular Duke and Dutchess of Perth, the Lord and Lady Ogilvie, and of Miss Florence M'Donald.

Printed for L. Gilliver. 368pp. 8vo. 1*s*. (Y)

Fictionalized memoirs of three of the most famous Scottish Jacobite ladies and their families, all of whom had close connections with the Young Pretender during the "'forty-five."

217. The gallant companion; or, an antidote for the hyp and vapours.

Printed for G. Woodfall, E. Withers, W. Reeves, etc. 331pp. 12mo. 3*s*. (I)

A miscellaneous collection of light pieces, including some brief amorous novels and *histoires*.

218. The life of Henry Simms, alias young gentleman Harry . . . all wrote by himself while under sentence of death in Newgate.

Printed for T. Parker and C. Corbett. 38pp. 8vo. (BM)

Ghost-written autogiography of a notorious robber and gamester hanged at Tyburn for his crimes.

219. _Memoirs of the most Christian-brute; or, the history of the late exploits of a certain great K——g_.
Printed for E. Pierce. 38, 70pp. 8vo. (Y)

a. 1747. Dublin. (Greenough).

A fierce satire of Louis XV of France, with special attention to his conduct of the War of the Austrian Succession, in which his country was England's chief enemy.

220. _Memoirs of the Nutrebian court: discovering the distresses of the queen, happy birth, and surprizing deliverance of her children_.
Printed for M. Laugham, J. Robinson, and W. Reeves. 2 vols. 12mo. 5_s_. (I; N)

An anonymous Jacobite's pseudo-orientalized, sentimental story of love, scandal, and political intrigue in a kingdom overrun by a usurper, but saved through the magical intervention of a sprite named Papaglia and his care of the rightful heirs, who finally regain the throne.

221. *The wanderer: or, surprizing escape. A narrative founded on true facts. . . . With some remarks on a romance called Ascanius.*
Printed for J. Robinson. 104pp. 4to. 1*s*.6*d*. (H)

A professed anti-Jacobite's rather sympathetic account of Prince Charles Edward Stuart's terrifying adventures in flight after the Battle of Culloden Moor. The author attacks John Burton's *Ascanius* (1746: above, No. 202) as a cruel vilification of the Young Chevalier.

222. Doddridge, Philip. *Some remarkable passages in the life of the Honourable Col. James Gardiner, who was slain at the Battle of Preston-Pans, 21st September, 1745.*
Printed for James Buckland and James Waugh. 260pp. 4to. (H; I; Y)

a. 1748. Printed for James Buckland and James Waugh. 271pp. 12mo. (Y)

This account of the great Christian soldier includes letters and other documents in support of its authenticity, but its record of Gardiner's conversion from apostasy to passionate faith is intensely imagined.

223. Fielding, Sarah. Familiar letters between the principal characters in David Simple.
Printed for the author and sold by A. Millar. 2 vols.
8vo. 10s. (H; I; N; P)

A miscellaneous gathering of essays and short epistolary tales having little to do with the novel itself (1744: above, No. 149). The Preface, and Letters XL-XLIV, were written by Henry Fielding.

*224. Harrington, James. The Oceana and other works of James Harrington Esq; . . . with an exact account of his life prefix'd by John Toland.
Third edition. Printed for A. Millar. 632pp. 4to. (C)
Oceana was first published in 1656 (Mish).

The Commonwealth of Oceana is the famous utopian political romance by a republican who was, despite his views, a good friend of Charles I. The volume also includes other political writings by Harrington.

225. Lawrence, John. Alexis, or the worthy unfortunate.
Printed for J. Cobham. 114pp. 8vo. 1s.6d. (BM)

a. 1748. Dublin: Printed by J. Kenneir. 50pp. 12mo. (Y)

A greatly reduced version of the original.

Fictionalized story of one Henry Sydenham of Manchester, who was ruined by the Jacobite uprising of 1745-1746.

226. Maxwell, John. The conversation: or, the lady's tale, a novel.
York: Printed for T. Gent. 36pp. 8vo. (H)

Brief sentimental tale of an amorous encounter, told in the form of a conversation between a young lady and her confidante.

*227. Midon, Francis. The history of Masianello.
Printed for Davis. 104pp. 12mo. 2s. (Y)

This native version was first published in 1729 (McBurney No. 117b).

This is the romantic story of the famous Italian fisherman Tommaso Aniello, who led the Neapolitans' revolt against the Spanish rulers in 1647, only to be assassinated, probably by his own followers.

228. Penrice, Gerard. A genuine and impartial account of the remarkable life and vicissitudes of fortune of Charles Ratcliffe, Esq.

Printed for the author. 182pp. 4to. 6d. (H)

An account of the checkered career of Ratcliffe (properly spelled Radcliffe), a participant in the Jacobite rebellion of 1715 who was exiled, but finally returned to England during the "'forty-five." He was executed at Tower Hill in December of 1746. The story of his brother the Earl of Derwentwater, who was hanged at the same place in 1716, is also included.

229. Richardson, Samuel. Clarissa, Or, the history of a young lady.

Printed for S. Richardson, 1747-1748. 7 vols. 12mo. 3s. per vol. (H; P; Y)

a. 1747-1749. Dublin: Printed for George Faulkner. (Sale).

b. 1749. Second edition. Printed for S. Richardson. 4 vols. 12mo. (Y)

Only four volumes were reprinted for the second edition; Richardson had anticipated the demand for a new edition, and printed enough copies of Vols. V-VII to meet it (Sale).

TRANSLATIONS

230. _Novellas espannolas. Or, moral and entertaining novels: translated from the original Spanish._
Printed for W. Reeve, J. Fox, and H. Cooke. 263pp. 12mo. 2_s_.6_d_. (N; LC)

A new collection of Spanish exemplary novels in the manner of Cervantes' _Novelas exemplares_ (see above, No. 124).

*231. Aesopus. _Fables of Aesop_.
Fifth edition. Printed for J. and R. Tonson, and J. Watts. 345pp. 12mo. (BM)

This version of Aesop, edited by Samuel Croxall, was first published c.1720.

See also above, Nos. 25, 68, and 122.

232. Argens, Jean Baptiste de Boyer, marquis d'. _New memoirs establishing a true knowledge of mankind, by_

discovering the affections of the heart, and the operations of the understanding in the various scenes of life. Printed for D. Browne, R. Hitt, and A. Millar. 2 vols. 8vo. (N)

Translated from Mémoires pour servir à l'histoire de l'esprit et du coeur (The Hague, 1744).

This collection includes brief novels of tender passion by "Mademoiselle Co**," along with essays and letters on subjects ranging from friendship to the cosmetic arts.

*233. Bidpai. The instructive and entertaining fables of Pilpay, an ancient Indian philosopher. Printed for S. Birt and D. Browne. 231pp. 12mo. 2s.6d. (I)

This version of Bidpai's fables was first published in 1679 (Conant).

See also above, No. 122.

a. 1743. (Conant).

According to Miss Conant the ancient Kalila and Dimna, from which these moralized oriental fables are drawn, had been known in England since medieval times.

234. Gellert, Christian Furchtegott. The life of the Countess of G . . . translated from the German by a lady. Printed for B. Law. 2 vols. 8vo. (P)

Translated from Leben der schwedischen Grafinn von G***.

An autobiographical epistolary novel about a Swedish Countess living in the joys of her impeccable virtue, which she (with her husband) displays at assemblies and balls in all the principal cities of Europe, much to the disadvantage of other ladies frequenting such places.

235. Prévost d'Exiles, Antoine Francois, Abbé. Memoirs of a man of honour. Translated from the French. Printed for J. Nourse. 2 vols. in 1. 12mo. 2s.6d. (H; N)

Translated from Mémoires d'un honnête homme, 1745.

A melancholy, allegedly autobiographical tale of a man of good family who succumbs to tempestuous passion, ruins his own life and that of a girl he loves, and finally comes to ultimate misery when he is thrown into prison.

1748

See also above, Nos. 32, 47, 49, 88, 97, 102, 136, 148, 150, 194, 200, 208, 222, and 225.

236. The agreeable medley; or, universal entertainer.
Printed for Malton. 8vo. (BM)

A miscellany of light poems and prose narratives, including several short novels and "histories."

237. An apology for the conduct of Mrs. Teresia Constantia Phillips.
Printed for the author, 1748-1749. 3 vols. 4to. (H)
See also below, Nos. 240 and 262.

Although told in the third person, this sensational account of one of the period's most notorious females is obviously based on autobiographical fact. According to Stauffer, it may have been dictated to one Paul Whitehead.

238. The entertaining travels and surprizing adventures of Mademoiselle de Leuirich. Who travelled over Europe, dressed in man's apparel, attend [sic] by her maid-servant as her valet de chambre.

2 vols. in 1. 12mo. (N)

A plagiarism of William Erskine's picaresque _Travels and adventures of Mademoiselle de Richelieu_ (1743: above, No. 118).

239. _The fortunate transport; or, the secret history of the life and adventures of the celebrated Polly Haycock, the lady of the gold watch. By a Creole_.
Printed for T. Taylor. 2 parts: 44, 45pp. 8vo. 1_s_. per part. (N)

A brief variation on Defoe's _Moll Flanders_ (see above, No. 52), this is the story of an unrepentant female picaro who was "begot by Chance, . . . nursed by Charity, brought up among Pickpockets, . . . and in spite of all that, now rolls in Ease, Splendor, and Luxury . . . ."

240. _The injured Iphigenia; a true history. In which the nature of libellous paragraphs, calculated to disturb the peace of families, is set in a proper light_.
27pp. 4to. 6_d_. (Y)

Apparently an answer to the Apology for the conduct of Mrs. Teresia Constantia Phillips (1748: above, No. 237).

241. Love and avarice; or, the fatal effects of preferring wealth to beauty. Exemplified in the history of a young gentleman . . . . By a lady of Shropshire.
Printed for T. Ward. 245pp. 8vo. (BM)

A sentimental novel about a love affair that ends tragically because of the greed and ambition of a foolish youth.

242. Mr. F——'s adventures in petticoats.
Printed for E. Penn. 3 parts. 2s.6d. (N)
Originally published in three parts as A spy on mother midnight; or, the templar metamorphos'd, 1748 (Listed in GM Feb., March, June 1748).

A quasi-pornographic epistolary narrative in which a spirited young templar named Richard, who is disguised as a female, writes to his friend Jack in town reporting what his special vantage point enables him to learn of country ladies, and what licentious fun he has with them.

*243. The unfortunate concubines: the history of fair Rosamond, mistress to Henry II. and Jane Shore, concubine to Edward IV. Kings of England.

Printed for R. Ware, C. Hitch, and J. Hodges. 165pp. 12mo. (N; P)

First published in 1720 (N).

Brief, romanticized narratives of the melancholy adventures of two of the most famous mistresses of English monarchs.

244. "Coetlogon, Denis de." Diogenes at court; or the modern cynic.

Printed for J. Jeffries. 62pp. 8vo. 1s. (I)

A satire of court life, and the conduct of the War of the Austrian Succession; professes to adopt the attitudes of the ancient Athenian sceptic.

*245. Berington, Simon. The adventures of Sig[r]. Gaudentio di Lucca.

Second edition. Printed for W. Innys, R. Manby, and H. S. Cox. 219pp. 8vo. (H; I; N)

First published in 1737 as The memoirs of . . . (McBurney No. 323).

A utopian voyage fiction displaying the virtues of an unknown African nation called Mezorania. Once thought to be the work of George Berkeley, _Gaudentio_ was enormously popular throughout most of the eighteenth century.

246. Cleland, John. _Fanny Hill; or, memoirs of a woman of pleasure. By a person of quality_.
Printed for G. Fenton, 1748-1749. 2 vols. 12mo. 3_s_. per vol. (Y)

This is the most famous English pornographic novel of the eighteenth century, written as a young girl's semi-epistolary autobiographical record of her introduction to love and prostitution.

247. Douglas, John. _The cornutor of seventy-five. Being a genuine narrative of the life . . . of Don Ricardo Honeywater . . . . Written originally in Spanish, by the author of Don Quixote_.
8vo. (BM)

a. 1748. Second edition. 8vo. (BM)

A vicious satire of Dr. Richard Mead (1653-1754), one of the greatest medical pioneers of the eighteenth century, and a learned man who gained the admiration of Dr. Johnson, among others.

248. Haywood, Eliza. Life's progress through the passions; or, the adventures of Natura. By the author of The fortunate foundlings.
Printed for T. Gardner. 231pp. 12mo. 2s.6d. (H; I; N; P; Y)

Mrs. Haywood's quasi-picaresque tale of a wayward youth who progressively indulges all the passions known to man, but finally gains wisdom and retires to a settled life.

249. Hervey, Lord John, of Ickworth. The court-spy; or, memoirs of St. J——m——s's. In a letter from a person of distinction in town, to his friend in Wales.
Printed for H. Carpenter. 45pp. 8vo. 1s. (H)

A short epistolary "spy" narrative satirizing the court of George II, written by one of its chief hangers-on.

250. Kelly, John. Memoirs of the life of John Medley, Esq; or, fortune reconcil'd to merit.
Printed for Fuller. 12mo. 2s.6d. (P; Y; LC)
A second volume of this work appeared in 1756, and the two were then combined and offered as two volumes in one.

The sentimental story of a male counterpart to Samuel Richardson's Pamela Andrews, written by the author of Pamela's conduct in high life (1741: above, No. 60), the best known of the spurious continuations of Richardson's novel.

251. Mitchell, M. Young Juba: or, the history of the Young Chevalier, from his birth, to his escape from Scotland, after the Battle of Culloden.
296pp. 12mo. (N)

A mildly sensational biographical account of Prince Charles Edward Stuart, written by one who claims companionship with his hero.

252. Pilkington, Letitia. Memoirs of Mrs. Laetitia Pilkington. Written by herself.

Dublin: Printed for the author. 2 vols. 12mo. (H)

a. 1748-1749. Dublin and London: Printed for R. Griffiths and G. Woodfall. 2 vols. 12mo. (H)

The sensational quasi-autobiographical apology for one of the period's most notorious females, who also includes little secret histories of famous people, living and dead, she claims to have known.

253. Smollett, Tobias. The adventures of Roderick Random. Printed for J. Osborn. 2 vols. 12mo. 6*s*. (H; P)

a. 1748. Second edition. Printed for J. Osborn. 2 vols. 12mo. (H)

254. Walcot, James. The new pilgrim's progress; or, the pious Indian convert. Containing a faithful account of Hattanii Gelashimen . . . who was baptiz'd into the Christian faith by the name of George James. 316pp. 12mo. (H)

a. 1749. Second edition. Printed for W. Owen. 316pp. 12mo. (BM)

A romanticized biographical treatment of a real man, who was best known in the period for the drama of his conversion and the devotion of his missionary excursions to minister to the Indians of South America.

255. Wyatt, James. The life and surprising adventures of James Wyatt, written by himself.
181pp. 8vo. (BM)

Defoesque fictionalized autobiography of a real-life English adventurer who, in two short years (1741-1743), was variously a mate on the privateer Revenge, a prisoner of war among the Spanish, a lost sailor in a tiny boat trying to get from the Canaries to Madeira, and a captive of the Barbary pirates and slave-traders.

TRANSLATIONS

256. Graffigny, Françoise d'Issembourg d'Happancourt de. Letters written by a Peruvian princess.
Printed for J. Brindley. 259pp. 12mo. 2s.6d. (H; Y)
Translated from Lettres d'une péruvienne, 1747.
See also below, No. 279, for the Sequel.

a. 1748. Dublin: Printed for Thomas Moore. 112pp. 12mo. (P)

b. 1749. Second edition. Printed for J. Brindley. 12mo. 2s.6d. (N)

Includes The sequel of the Peruvian letters.

Mme. de Graffigny's imitation of Montesquieu's Lettres persanes (1721) presents thirty-eight letters supposedly written by Zilia, a young Peruvian "virgin of the sun" rescued from Spanish invaders and brought to Paris, where she is permitted to view French life with innocent detachment. A keen observer, Zilia is also a lonely disappointed lover, whose commentaries on French society are delivered in letters addressed to her beloved young Peruvian Aza, a captive of the Spanish.

*257. Marana, Giovanni Paolo. Letters writ by a Turkish spy, who lived five and forty years, undiscovered, at Paris. Twelfth edition. Printed for A. Wilde. 8 vols. 12mo. 1L. (H)

The early volumes of this translation were first published in 1687 (P).

Translated from L'espion turc, 1684.

Marana's work, which presents the "spy" Mahmut's letters home to Turkey, launched a long series of similar narratives focusing on an alien's satirical observations on the customs, morals, and institutions of the host society. The original six volumes of 1684 were later expanded by English and French writers and editors.

1749

See also above, Nos. 90, 100, 120, 123, 127, 146, 178, 229, 254, and 256.

258. Adventures of Melinda; a lady of distinction, now living.

Printed for H. Carpenter. 59pp. 8vo. 1s. (Bro)

A secret history of contemporary high life, "Founded on real, authentic Facts."

259. The amours of Don Carlos. A true history, translated from a manuscript privately handed about at the French court.

Printed for R. Freeman. 139pp. 8vo. 2s. (N; Pri; UCLA)

A secret history of Prince Charles Edward Stuart's love affairs, most of them probably invented by the anonymous author himself. The work only glances at the "'forty-five."

260. An authentick account of the conduct of the Young Chevalier.
Printed for Nutt, Dodd, Barnes, etc. 43pp. 8vo. (H)

Romanticized narrative of Prince Charles Edward Stuart's adventures in England and Scotland from the time of his arrival from France in 1745, until the end of his flight after the Battle of Culloden in 1746.

261. An authentick account of the life of Paul Wells, gent. who was eexecuted [sic] at Oxford, Sept. 1, 1749, for forgery. . . . By a gentleman of C. C. C. Oxon.
Printed for R. Baldwin. 27pp. 4to. 6d. (Y)

A slightly sentimentalized, but otherwise quite routinely sensational criminal "life." The real-life subject, a gifted and successful young attorney, sank to embezzlement and was finally condemned for changing a "2" to a "3" on a receipt.

262. A counter-apology: or, genuine confession. Being a caution to the fair sex in general. Containing the secret history, amours, and intrigues, of M—— P——, a famous British courtezan.
61pp. 8vo. 1s. (N)

A spurious narrative response to the Apology for the conduct of Mrs. Teresia Constantia Phillips (1748-1749: above, No. 237). Pretends to be a defense against the public "vilification" pronounced by the Apology, but actually charges "Constantia" with whoredom in a titillating account of her life and adventures.

263. The French-bite: or the genuine narrative of the exploits of the Marquis Del-Bruce.
Printed for W. Webb. 31pp. 12mo. (H)

Allegedly taken from the mouth of its subject's servant, this pamphlet details the escapades of a real French impostor who, during six weeks of the year 1749, managed to bilk numerous London businessmen and even to be feted at Court.

264. The history of the human heart: or, the adventures of a young gentleman.

Printed for J. Freeman. 314pp. 12mo. 3s. (N; P)

A pornographic narrative by an author whose magical "second sight" allows him to see the whole private life of his hero Camillo. The focus is on Camillo's sexual experience, beginning in the womb, and the "learned" text is accompanied by pretentious footnotes.

*265. The history of Valentine and Orson, the two sons of the emperor of Greece.

Dublin. 98pp. 8vo. (BM)

First printed c.1565 (Y).

A condensed version of the old romantic adventure story about a heroic youth and his brother, a "wild man of the woods," and the scrapes (sometimes comic, sometimes melodramatic) their differing natures get them into.

266. The ladies advocate: or, wit and beauty a match for treachery and inconstancy.

Printed for C. Long. 304pp. 12mo. 3s. (Y)

An alleged secret history of contemporary high life, "Digested in the Manner of a Novel," and containing a series of "Gallantries, Intrigues, and Amours, Fortunate and Sinister."

267. <u>The royal African: or, memoirs of the young prince of Annamaboe</u>.
Printed for W. Reeve, G. Woodfall, and J. Barnes. 53pp. 4to. (Y)
See also below, Nos. B27 and B36.

This anti-slavery attack on the Royal African Company fictionalizes the adventures of a visiting African Prince whose father was persuaded to allow him to journey first to France, where he was treated royally, and then to England, where he was sold into slavery by a corrupt sea-captain.

268. <u>Satan's harvest home: or the present state of whorecraft</u>.
Printed for the editor. 62pp. 8vo. 1<u>s</u>. (BM)

A series of pornographic episodes from imaginary memoirs allegedly written by a comrade of a whoremonger, "the Hon. Jack S**n**r."

269. "Philomath, S. F." The petticoat-pensioners: being memoirs of the most remarkable of those gentlemen, in and about London and Westminster.
Printed for J. Horner. 204pp. 8vo. (BM)

Brief, salacious narrative sketches of contemporary low-life, with emphasis on imaginary pimps and gigolos.

*270. Aubin, Penelope. The life of Madam de Beaumont, a French lady.
56pp. 12mo. (Y)
First published in 1721 (McBurney No. 119).

a. 1741. (NCBEL).

Mrs. Aubin's important early novel combines a spirit of pious exhortation, the excitement of Defoesque travel adventure, and the attractions of a conventional story of love and exalting marriage.

271. Carew, Bampfylde-Moore. An apology for the life of Bampfylde-Moore Carew, . . . king of the beggars and dog merchant-general.
Printed for W. Owen. 151pp. 8vo. (C)

See also above, No. 167.

A new fictionalized version of the life of the celebrated "gypsy."

272. Fielding, Henry. *The history of Tom Jones, a foundling.*
Printed for A. Millar. 6 vols. 12mo. 3*s*. per vol. (I; P; Y)

a. 1749. Second edition. Printed for A. Millar. 6 vols. 12mo. (I; P; Y)
Cross calls this the second edition, though it is not so named.

b. 1749. Third edition. Printed for A. Millar. 4 vols. 12mo. (I; Y)
Cross calls this the third edition, though it is not so named.

c. 1749. Dublin: Printed for John Smith. 3 vols. 12mo. (I; Y)

273. Fielding, Sarah. *The governess; or, the little female academy.*

Printed for the author. 245pp. 12mo. 2s.6d. (H; P)

a. 1749. Second edition. Printed for A. Millar. 146pp. 12mo. (I)

This "history of Mrs. Teachum and her nine girls," a gathering of moral fairy tales for children and adolescents, was the most popular of Miss Fielding's works in the eighteenth century.

274. Haywood, Eliza [?]. Dalinda: or, the double marriage. Being the genuine history of a very recent, and interesting adventure.
Printed for T. Corbett and G. Woodfall. 288pp. 12mo. 3d. (I; N; P)
Not certainly by Mrs. Haywood (Whicher).

A domestic novel of amorous intrigue and false marriage, probably based on the real affair between a Mr. Cresswell and Miss Scrope.

275. ———. Epistles for the ladies.
Printed for T. Gardner. 2 vols. 8vo. 2s. (C; I)

Brief, discontinuous narrative epistles by exemplary female characters with romantic names like Aminta, Isabinda, and Sophronia, all of whom display a piety and sobriety quite unknown in the early amorous novels of Mrs. Haywood.

TRANSLATIONS

*276. Aulnoy, Marie Catherine Jumelle de Berneville, comtesse d'. A collection of novels and tales of the fairies.
Third edition. Printed for J. Brotherton, W. Meadows, R. Ware, etc. 3 vols. 12mo. 7s.6d. (H)

This translation was first published in 1707 (McBurney No. 27).

Translated from Nouvelles espanolles, 1692, and Contes des fées, 1698.

Contains Mme. d'Aulnoy's oriental fairy tales and her imitations of Cervantes' exemplary novels.

277. Crébillon, Claude Prosper Jolyot de. The amours of Zeokinizal king of the Kofiranis. Translated from the Arabic of the famous traveller Krinelbol: with a key.
Printed for G. Smith. 95pp. 8vo. 1s.6d. (Y)

Translated from Les amours de Zeokinizul, roi des Kofirans, 1746.

Licentious orientalized satire of Louis XV and the mistresses who preceded the arrival of Mme. de Pompadour.

*278. Gueulette, Thomas Simon. Peruvian tales, related, in one thousand and one hours, by one of the select virgins of Cusco, to the Ynca of Peru, to dissuade him from a resolution he had taken to destroy himself by poison. Printed for J. Hodges. 4 vols. 12mo. (Y)

The original Vols. I and II, translated by Samuel Humphreys, were first published in 1734 (McBurney No. 294); Vols. III and IV are a spurious continuation by John Kelly, and were added in 1739 and 1744, respectively.

Translated from Les mille et une heure, contes péruviens, 1733-1734.

a. 1742. Vol. III. Printed for J. Robinson. 280pp. 12mo. 3s. (Listed in GM May 1742).

b. 1744. Vol. IV. Printed for E. Curll. 12mo. 4s. (Listed in GM Sept. 1744).

c. 1745. Second edition. Printed for E. Curll. 4 vols. 12mo. 13*s*. (Straus).

Like Gueulette's *Chinese tales* (see above, No. 29) and *Mogul tales* (see above, No. 128), this is a pseudo-oriental imitation of the *Arabian nights* (see above, No. 179).

279. Hugary de Lamarche-Courmont, Ignace. *Sequel of the letters written by a Peruvian princess*.
Dublin: Printed by R. Jones. 31pp. 12mo. (P)
Translated from *Lettres d'Aza ou d'un péruvien* (Amsterdam, 1749).
See above, No. 256, for Mme. de Graffigny's original work, with which this *Sequel* was usually printed from 1749 on.

a. 1749. *Supplement to the letters, written by a Peruvian princess*.
Printed for J. Brindley. 6*d*. (Listed in *GM* Jan. 1749).

b. 1749. Included in *Letters written by a Peruvian princess*, second edition (see above, No. 256b).

The letters in the _Sequel_ are all by Aza, and are addressed to his beloved Zilia, heroine of Mme. de Graffigny's _Peruvian princess_. Their main purpose is to explain his conversion to Catholicism, and his subsequent betrothal to a Spanish lady.

280. Le Sage, Alain René. _The adventures of Gil Blas of Santillane_.

Printed for J. Osborn. 4 vols. 12mo. 8_s_. (Y)

A new translation by Tobias Smollett.

See also above, No. 105.

(For the original publication of the first English translation, see McBurney No. 85.)

281. Voltaire, François Marie Arouet de. _Zadig, or the book of fate_.

Printed for John Brindley. 238pp. 12mo. 2_s_.6_d_. (I)

Translated from _Zadig, ou la destinée. Histoire orientale_, 1748.

This is the first of Voltaire's orientalized philosophical romances.

Appendix A

Unverified Editions of Authentic Works

1740

*A1. Chetwood, William Rufus. The voyages, travels and adventures of William Owen Gwin Vaughan, Esq.; with the history of his brother Jonathan Vaughan, six years a slave in Tunis.
2 vols. 12mo. (Advertised by Osborn in Gueulette's Chinese tales, 1740.)
First published in 1736 (McBurney No. 312).

A Defoesque imaginary voyage which, however, anticipates the plot of Tobias Smollett's The adventures of Roderick Random (1748: above, No. 253) in some striking ways.

*A2. Croxall, Samuel, ed. A select collection of novels and histories. By several eminent hands.
Second edition. 6 vols. (Advertised by Osborn in Gueulette's Chinese tales, 1740).

First published in 1720-1722 (McBurney No. 117).

Croxall's collection includes dozens of novels mostly from established Continental genres such as the picaresque romance, the Italian *novella*, the Spanish exemplary novel, and the French *nouvelle*. Mme. de La Fayette, Machiavelli, Cervantes, and Le Sage are all well represented.

TRANSLATIONS

A3. Bandello, Matteo. *The novels of Bandello. Translated from the Italian*.
4 vols. 4to. (Greenough).
Translated from *Novelliere*, 1554.

Matteo Bandello was one of the greatest and most prolific practitioners of the art of the Italian *novella*, and his work was exceedingly popular in England from the sixteenth-century onward.

*A4. Fénelon, François de Salignac de La Mothe. *The tales and fables of the late Archbishop of Cambray, author of Telemachus, in French and English, written originally for the institution of a young prince*.

(Advertised by Osborn in Gueulette's _Chinese tales_, 1740.)

This translation was first published in 1729 as _Twenty seven tales and fables, . . . invented for the education of a Prince, by the late Archbishop of Cambray_ (I).

A5. Mouhy, Charles de Fieux, chevalier de. _The memoirs of Anna Maria de Moras, Countess of Corbon._
Printed for T. Cooper. 1_s_.6_d_. (Listed in _LM_ Dec. 1740).

Translated from _Mémoires d'Anne-Marie, comtesse de Courbon_ (The Hague, 1739).

A sentimental novel in imitation of Marivaux's _La vie de Marianne_, 1731-1741 (see above, No. 77).

1741

*A6. _Complete history of the right villainous John Hall, the late famous and notorious robber. Penn'd from his own mouth some time before his death._
(Chandler).

First published in 1704 as _Memoirs of the right villainous John Hall . . ._ (Stauffer).

A routine fictionalized biography of a glamorous criminal.

*A7. Grainger, Lydia. New court tales.
Printed for E. Curll. 2s.6d. (Straus).

Apparently a new edition of, or an addition to, Modern amours; or, a secret history of the adventures of some persons of the first rank, 1733 (McBurney No. 283).

Modern amours is a collection of ten domestic novels of love and intrigue, all purporting to treat of affairs in high life.

TRANSLATIONS

*A8. Le Sage, Alain René. The bachelor of Salamanca; or, memoirs of Don Cherubim de la Ronda, Vol. II.
Printed for C. Hitch and G. Hawkins. (Listed in GM May 1741).

This translation, by John Lockman, was first published in two volumes in 1737-1739 (McBurney No. 324).

Translated from Le bachelier de Salamanque, 1736-1738.

1742

*A9. <u>The travels of an English gentleman from London to Rome on foot; . . . likewise the debauched lives and amorous intrigues of the priests and nuns</u>.
Fourth edition. (Greenough).
An alleged fifth edition was published in 1728 (Y).

Anti-Catholic diatribe, rendered in the form of a travel narrative interlarded with episodes of scandalous amours in European churches, convents, and monasteries.

TRANSLATIONS

*A10. Vignancourt, Adrien de la Vieuville d'Orville, comte de. <u>The tragical history of the Chevalier de Vaudray and the Countess de Vergi. In two parts. To which is annexed a short novel, entitled, The inhuman husband</u>.
(Greenough).
This translation, by James Morgan, was first published in 1726 (McBurney No. 202).
Translated from <u>La Comtesse de Vergi, nouvelle historique, galante, & tragique</u>, 1722.

A melancholy, sentimental love story of two virtuous French aristocrats.

1743

*A11. The nunnery tales; or the amours of the priests and nuns.

Printed for T. Davis, and published in parts. (Wiles).

First published in 1727 (McBurney No. 219).

Secret histories of scandalous affairs in churches and monasteries.

*A12. The pleasures of matrimony, with a variety of merry and delightful stories.

Printed for J. Clarke. 8vo. (Greenough).

First published in 1688 (H).

A group of jocular domestic tales specifically celebrating the joys of virtuous married life.

*A13. Barker, Jane. The entertaining novels of Mrs. Jane Barker.

8vo. (Greenough).

This collection was first published in 1719 (McBurney No. 95).

Includes her didactic romances Love's intrigues; or, the history of the amours of Bosvil and Galesin (1713: McBurney No. 66) and Exilius: or, the banish'd Roman (1715: McBurney No. 78).

*A14. Overbury, Thomas. An account of the trial and execution of Joan Perry and her 2 sons for the supposed murder of Mr. Harrison.

Printed for Wilford. 2d. (Listed in GM May 1743).

First published in 1676 as A true and perfect account of the examination, confession, trial, condemnation and execution of Joan Perry and her two sons (C).

A very brief, vividly dramatic record of a sensational crime.

1744

*A15. Manley, Mary de la Rivière. Memoirs of the life of Mrs. Mary Manley, author of the Atalantis.

Printed for J. Robinson. (Greenough).

First published in 1714 as The adventures of Rivella (McBurney No. 72).

This is Mrs. Manley's fictionalized autobiography.

TRANSLATIONS

A16. Cervantes Saavedra, Miguel de. The history of the renowned Don Quixote de la Mancha.

Printed for J. Cooke. 2 vols. (Putnam).

According to Putnam, this is an abridged translation by Charles Henry Wilmot.

See also above, Nos. 27, 100, and 123.

1745

TRANSLATIONS

A17. Le Sage, Alain René. <u>Une journée des parques: a day's work of the Fates</u>.
Cambridge: Printed for Charles Bathurst. 30pp. 8vo.
(Greenough).
Extracted and translated from <u>Histoire de Gil Blas de Santillane</u>, 1715-1735 (see above, No. 105).

1746

*A18. Gwinnett, Richard, and Elizabeth Thomas. <u>Pylades and Corinna: or, memoirs of the lives, amours, and writings of Richard Gwinnett Esq . . . and Mrs. Elizabeth Thomas Junr</u>.
Second edition. Printed for E. Curll. 2 vols. 8vo.
10*s*. (Straus).
First published in 1731-1732 (McBurney No. 259).

A narrative which fictionalizes the romantic lives of two apparently real people who carried on a love affair of sixteen years duration; their tender letters and amatory verses are the focus of these volumes.

1749

TRANSLATIONS

*A19. Galland, Antoine. Arabian nights entertainments: consisting of 1,001 stories told by the sultaness of the Indies, to divert the sultan.

Ninth edition. 8 vols. 12mo. (Greenough).

This translation was first published in 1706-1717 (McBurney No. 23).

See also above, No. 179.

Appendix B

Unauthenticated Titles

1740

B1. *A Chinese tale.*

Printed for J. Cooper. (Listed in *GM* Feb. 1740).

B2. *The ghost and the miller. A merry tale.*

6*d*. (Listed in *LM* May 1740).

B3. *The history of Adam and Eve.*

Printed for O. Payne. Folio. 1*s*.6*d*. (Listed in *GM* July 1740).

B4. *The history of the life and death of David, with moral reflections.*

Printed for E. Curll. 3*s*.6*d*. (Listed in *GM* Aug. 1740).

*B5. Venetian tales: or, a curious collection of entertaining novels and diverting tales. Chiefly designed for the amusement of the fair sex.
Second edition. Printed for J. and J. Fox. 243pp. 12mo. (Greenough).

Probably first published in 1737 (McBurney No. X45).

B6. The whimsical apothecary: a secret history.
(Advertised in Eliza Haywood's The city jilt, 1740.

B7. Winter evening's entertainment.
Printed for T. Wright and S. Birt. 8vo. 5s. (Listed in GM Nov. 1740).

B8. The world in miniature; or, the entertaining traveller.
Printed for Corbet. 5s. (Listed in GM May 1740).

1741

B9. <u>A genuine history of Thomas Kouli Kan</u>.
Printed for A. Dodd. 1<u>s</u>.6<u>d</u>. (Listed in <u>GM</u> Oct. 1741).
See also below, No. B10.

Allegedly a translation from the Dutch, this was probably an adaptation of <u>The history of Thomas Kouli Kan</u> (1740: above, No. 10).

B10. <u>The life of Thomas Kula Kan</u>.
Printed for Wilcocks. 6<u>d</u>. (Listed in <u>GM</u> Oct. 1741).

Like No. B9, above, this was probably an adaptation of <u>The history of Thomas Kouli Kan</u> (1740: above, No. 10).

B11. <u>Menander and Aurelia; or, the triumphs of love and constancy: a novel</u>.
Printed for Milles. 6<u>d</u>. (Listed in <u>GM</u> Sept. 1741).

TRANSLATIONS

B12. <u>Spanish amusements: being a curious collection of fifteen novels. Translated . . . by Mr. Ozell</u>.
2 vols. 7<u>s</u>. (Straus).

1742

B13. *Italian love: or, eunuchism displayed. Describing all the different kinds of eunuchs . . . . Written by a person of honour*.
(Greenough).

1743

B14. *Three more political fables*.
Printed for M. Cooper. 1*s*. (Listed in *GM* April 1743).
See also below, No. B15.

B15. *Two political fables*.
Printed for Cooper. 6*d*. (Listed in *GM* Feb. 1743).
See also above, No. B14.

B16. *A voyage to Ipswich*.
Printed for Roberts. 1*s*. (Listed in *GM* April 1743).

1744

B17. Cupid's tales; or, the fortunate lovers. Illustrated in 8 novels.

Printed for Cooper. 1s.6d. (Listed in GM Nov. 1744).

B18. Collyer, Mary [?]. A Christmas-box for masters and misses; consisting of stories proper to improve the minds of children.

Printed for Collyer. 6d. (Listed in GM Dec. 1744).

See also below, No. B37.

1745

B19. The illustrious unfortunate; or, the adventures of great heroes.

Printed for Noble. 2s.6d. (Listed in GM May 1745).

B20. Jacky Nory's book of stories.

Printed for Corbet. 6d. (Listed in GM June 1745).

B21. <u>A third collection of classics</u>.
Printed for J. Brindley. 12s.6d. (Listed in GM May 1745).

B22. <u>Veillée à la campagne; or, the semnel. A tale</u>.
Printed for Manby and Cox. 1s. (Listed in GM May 1745).

1746

B23. <u>Love and loyalty; or, the generous deceit. A true story</u>.
Printed for W. Reeve. 6d. (Listed in GM Oct. 1746).

B24. <u>Select fables</u>.
Printed for Osberne. 2 vols. 3s. (Listed in GM Oct. 1746).

1747

B25. *Entertaining fables for little masters and misses.* 4*d*. (Listed in *GM* May 1747).

B26. *Twenty moral fables, with a dissertation on fables.* Printed for Robinson. 1*s*. (Listed in *GM* Dec. 1747).

1749

B27. *The African prince, now in England, to Zara at his father's court.*
Printed for Payne and Bouquet. 6*d*. (Listed in *GM* July 1749).
See also above, No. 267, and below, No. B36.

B28. *Engaging and instructive histories: comprehending a variety of the most extraordinary and moving events, of incontestable authority.*
Printed for R. Spavan. 2 vols. 12mo. (Greenough).

B29. Heroic virtue; or, the noble sufferers. Exemplified in the illustrious lives . . . of several noblemen and ladies.
8vo. (Greenough).

B30. Instructive histories.
2 vols. 12mo. 6s. (Listed in GM Nov. 1749).

B31. The marriage of the devil. A novel.
Printed for Owen. 6d. (Listed in GM Jan. 1749).

B32. Memoirs of an unhappy old gentlewoman.
Printed for Cooper. 1s. (Listed in GM Feb. 1749).
See also below, No. B33.

B33. The memoirs of another unhappy old gentleman.
Printed for Cooper. 1s. (Listed in LM Feb. 1749).
See also above, No. B32.

B34. Memoirs of the life of Mrs. A——a W——t.
Printed for Reeve. 1s. (Listed in LM Dec. 1749).

B35. New tale of a tub.

Printed for A. Dodd. 6d. (Listed in GM March 1749).

B36. Zara, at the Court of Annamaboe, to the African prince, now in England.

Printed for Payne and Bouquet. 6d. (Listed in GM Aug. 1749).

See also above, Nos. 267 and B27.

B37. Collyer, Mary. The Christmas-box.

Printed for Payne and Bouquet. 2 vols. 1s. (Listed in GM Dec. 1749).

See also above, No. B18.

TRANSLATIONS

B38. The life of Cleopatra, queen of Egypt. Translated from the Italian. Written by a nobleman.

Printed for M. Cooper. (Greenough).

Bibliography

Adams, P. G. Travelers and Travel-Liars, 1660-1800. Berkeley and Los Angeles: University of California Press, 1962.

Anderson, Paul B. "Delarivière Manley's Prose Fiction." PQ, 13 (April 1934), 168-188.

————. "Mistress Delarivière Manley's Biography." MP, 33 (1936), 261-262.

Anderson, P. J. A Note on Dr. John Burton's Ascanius; or, the Young Adventurer (1747), in N & Q, Twelfth Ser., 12 (Jan.-June 1923), 172.

Baker, Sheridan. "Henry Fielding's The Female Husband: Fact and Fiction." PMLA, 74 (June 1959), 213-224.

Block, Andrew. The English Novel, 1740-1850: A Catalogue. London: William Dawson and Sons, 1961.

Boyce, Benjamin, ed. The Adventures of Lindamira, A Lady of Quality. Minneapolis: University of Minnesota Press, 1949.

British Museum General Catalogue of Printed Books.

The Cambridge Bibliography of English Literature, ed. F. W. Bateson. 4 vols. Cambridge: The University Press, 1941.

Chandler, Frank Wadleigh. The Literature of Roguery. 2 vols. Boston: Houghton, Mifflin and Company, 1907.

Conant, Martha Pike. The Oriental Tale in England in the Eighteenth Century. New York: Columbia University Press, 1908.

Cox, Edward Godfrey. A Reference Guide to the Literature of Travel. 3 vols. Seattle: University of Washington Press, 1935-1949.

Cross, Wilbur L. The History of Henry Fielding. 3 vols. New Haven: Yale University Press, 1917-1919.

Day, Robert Adams. Told in Letters: Epistolary Fiction before Richardson. Ann Arbor: University of Michigan Press, 1966.

Ellison, Lee M. "Gaudentio di Lucca: A Forgotten Utopia." PMLA, 50 (1935), 494-509.

English Prose Fiction, 1700-1800, in the University of Illinois Library, ed. William Harlin McBurney. Urbana: University of Illinois Press, 1965.

English Fiction to 1820 in the University of Pennsylvania Library, ed. Sidney Gecker. Philadelphia: University of Pennsylvania Press, 1954.

Erickson, James P. "The Novels of Eliza Haywood." Unpublished doctoral dissertation, University of Minnesota, 1961.

Esdaile, Arundell. _A List of English Tales and Prose Romances Printed before 1740_. London: The Bibliographical Society, 1912.

Fielding, Henry. _The Female Husband and Other Writings_, ed. Claude E. Jones. Liverpool: English Reprints Series, 1961.

Foster, James R. "The Abbé Prévost and the English Novel." _PMLA_, 42 (1927), 443-464.

The Gentleman's Magazine, 1731-51: The Lists of books, collected with annual indexes and the index to the first twenty years compiled by Edward Kimber (1752). London: Gregg-Archive (English Bibliographical Sources, Ser. 1, No. 6), 1966.

Gove, Philip Babcock. The Imaginary Voyage in Prose Fiction: A History of Its Criticism and a Guide for Its Study, with an Annotated Check List of 215 Imaginary Voyages from 1700 to 1800. New York: Columbia University Press, 1941.

Greenough, C. N. "Catalogue of English Prose Fiction, 1470-1832" (a card-index in Harvard University's Widener Library).

Haas, Gaylord R. "The English Novel from 1731 to 1740: A Decade Study." Unpublished doctoral dissertation, Northwestern University, 1966.

Halkett, Samuel, and John Laing. Dictionary of Anonymous and Pseudonymous English Literature. New ed. 9 vols. Edinburgh: Oliver and Boyd, 1926-1962.

Hannay, David. Life and Writings of Tobias George Smollett. With a Bibliography compiled by John P. Anderson of the British Museum. London: The Walter Scott Publishing Company, [1887].

Haviland, Thomas Philip. "The 'Roman de Longue Haleine' on English Soil." Unpublished doctoral dissertation, University of Pennsylvania, 1931.

Heidler, Joseph Bunn. _The History, from 1700-1800, of English Criticism of Prose Fiction_. Urbana: University of Illinois Studies in Language and Literature, 13, No. 2 (May 1928).

Hughes, Helen Sard. "The Life and Works of Mary Mitchell Collyer." Unpublished doctoral dissertation, University of Chicago, 1917.

———. "Translations of the Vie de Marianne and their Relation to Contemporary English Fiction." _MP_, 15 (1917), 491-512.

Hutchins, Henry Clinton. _Robinson Crusoe and its Printing, 1719-1731: A Bibliographical Study_. New York: Columbia University Press, 1925.

Irwin, William Robert. _The Making of 'Jonathan Wild': A Study in the Literary Method of Henry Fielding_. New York: Columbia University Press, 1941.

Jones, S. Paul. _A List of French Prose Fiction from 1700 to 1750_. New York: H. W. Wilson Company, 1939.

Kreissman, Bernard. _Pamela-Shamela: A Study of the criticisms, burlesques, parodies, and adaptations of Richardson's 'Pamela'_. Lincoln: Bison Books of the University of Nebraska Press, 1960.

The London Magazine, Vols. 9-18 (1740-1749).

Longaker, Mark. English Biography in the Eighteenth Century. Philadelphia: University of Pennsylvania Press, 1931.

Major, John Campbell. The Role of Personal Memoirs in English Biography and Novel. Philadelphia: University of Pennsylvania Press, 1934.

Mayo, Robert D. The English Novel in the Magazines, 1740-1815: With a Catalogue of 1375 Magazine Novels and Novelettes. Evanston: Northwestern University Press, 1962.

McBurney, William Harlin. A Check List of English Prose Fiction, 1700-1739. Cambridge: Harvard University Press, 1960.

McKillop, Alan Dugald. "English Circulating Libraries, 1725-1750." The Library, Fourth Ser., 14 (1934), 477-485.

Mish, Charles C. English Prose Fiction, 1600-1700: A Chronological Checklist. Charlottesville: Bibliographical Society of the University of Virginia, 1967.

Moore, John Robert. A Checklist of the Writings of Daniel Defoe. Bloomington: Indiana University Press, 1960.

Morgan, Charlotte E. The Rise of the Novel of Manners: A Study of English Prose Fiction between 1600 and 1740. New York: Columbia University Press, 1911.

The New Cambridge Bibliography of English Literature, Vol. II: 1660-1800, ed. George Watson. Cambridge: The University Press, 1971.

Plant, Marjorie. The English Book Trade: An Economic History of the Making and Sale of Books. London: George Allen and Unwin, 1939.

Putnam, Samuel. "Translator's Introduction" and "Bibliography" to The Ingenious Gentleman Don Quixote de la Mancha, by Miguel de Cervantes Saavedra. New York: Viking Press, 1949.

Richetti, John J. Popular Fiction Before Richardson: Narrative Patterns, 1700-1739. Oxford: The Clarendon Press, 1969.

Sale, William M., Jr. Samuel Richardson: A Bibliographical Record of His Literary Career with Historical Notes. New Haven: Yale University Press, 1936.

The Scots Magazine, Vols. 2-11 (1740-1749).

Singer, Godfrey Frank. The Epistolary Novel: Its Origin, Development, Decline, and Residuary Influence. Philadelphia: University of Pennsylvania Press, 1933.

Stauffer, Donald A. The Art of Biography in Eighteenth Century England, with a Bibliographical Supplement. Princeton: Princeton University Press, 1941.

Straus, Ralph. The Unspeakable Curll: Being Some Account of Edmund Curll, Bookseller: To Which Is Added a Full List of His Books. London: Chapman and Hall, 1927.

Teerink, Herman. A Bibliography of the Writings of Jonathan Swift. 2nd ed., ed. Arthur H. Scouten. Philadelphia: University of Pennsylvania Press, 1963.

Tucker, Joseph. "On the Authorship of The Turkish Spy." PBSA, 53 (1958), 34-47.

Werner, Herman Oscar, Jr. "The Life and Works of Sarah Fielding." Unpublished doctoral dissertation, Harvard University, 1939.

Whicher, George Frisbie. The Life and Romances of Mrs. Eliza Haywood. New York: Columbia University Press, 1915.

Wiles, Roy McKeen. _Serial Publication in England before 1750_. Cambridge: The University Press, 1957.

Index

Reference is to item numbers.